Historic Fife Murde
at Falkland, St Andrews & Magus

JOURNEYS THROUGH FIFE BETWEEN FORTH AND TAY

Falkland Palace, summer 2001.

The Bishop's Bridge at Ceres, May 2002.

Historic Fife Murders

at Falkland, St Andrews & Magus Muir

JOURNEYS THROUGH FIFE BETWEEN FORTH AND TAY

by Duncan Glen

Akros Publications

First published 2002 by
AKROS PUBLICATIONS
33 Lady Nairn Avenue, Kirkcaldy, Fife, Scotland
copyright © text and photographs Duncan Glen 2002
Typeset by Emtext [Scotland] Printed in Scotland
ISBN 0 86142 135 3

Title-page illustration: Bishop's Wood near Magus Muir,
west of St Andrews. Photograph by the author 2002.

Falkland Palace, June 2002.

Contents

View of East Lomond over Balbirnie House, Markinch, May 1998.

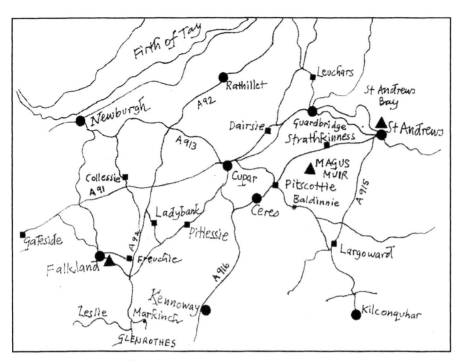

Sketch map, partly diagrammatic.

Dairsie Church as seen in April 2002 from the old Dairsie Bridge which crosses the Eden below the church. April 2002. As ROBERT LOUIS STEVENSON wrote, "All I seek, the heaven above, / And the road below me" and to WALT WHITMAN,

The paths worn in the irregular hollows by the road sides!
I believe you are latent with unseen existences . . .

Preface and Acknowledgements

IN MAKING these journeys through Fife I began by following the routes taken by the men and women involved in these murders but, of course, I could not resist making some detours and allowing curiosity to take me into places and situations that were off the tracks beaten by the fanatics who would not in those days appreciate natural scenery. Also, obviously, unlike these men and women who rode through Fife by the routes I have described in this book, I enjoyed the comfort of modern roads and tended to venture out on sunny days. Indeed, although the events described here are clearly far from being as festive as David Wilkie's celebratory "Pitlessie Fair", making this book has been a pleasure, as were the journeys through Fife that I took when writing my *Illustrious Fife* and which made writing this book much easier. However, in taking and presenting the photographs that illustrate these journeys I have tried not to forget that some beautiful places were scenes of dark deeds.

All histories, not least official ones, are to some extent a fiction and I have not burdened readers with over-many qualifying phrases to indicate that I may be giving a view of what happened that is not provable beyond reasonable doubt. Despite the popular acceptance of the story told in Sir Walter Scott's *The Fair Maid of Perth*, we can never know if the Duke of Rothesay died of starvation or dysentery. Similarly we do not know what *exactly* happened in Cardinal Beaton's room when he was assassinated, or on Magus Muir when Archbishop James Sharp's daughter, Isabel, witnessed her father's murder. The scene as described by Isabel's brother, Sir William Sharp, is inevitably a different one from that described by James Russell of Kettle, who was one of the assassins. This is so even in details of what the murderers took from the Archbishop's body and coach, far less in emotional content. I may aim for impartiality, but my view has been influenced by my boyhood having been spent in Covenanting Lanarkshire where the Presbyterian martyrs were venerated for their courage as much as for their faith. Of course these Covenanters were as much fanatics and fundamentalists as Cardinal David Beaton and King Charles II, beside whom Archbishop James Sharp was a weak fellow-traveller. The Duke of Rothesay must remain an unknown quantity, but Robert Stewart, first Duke of Albany, was as power-mad as any of the later Stewarts, including Charles I and II and the so-called Bonnie Prince who wantonly led so many Highlanders to their deaths.

With regard to the murder of Cardinal David Beaton, many Presbyterians have thought that the "loon was well away" whilst also agreeing with Sir David Lindsay that "the deed was foully done." The murder of Archbishop Sharp increased the fanaticism of both the extreme Covenanters and those who served the government, but it did not fundamentally alter the course of British history. Like so many of the Acts of the modern Westminster Parliament, the removal of King James VII in 1688 was decided by English opinion and not by what Scottish Covenanters had fought and died for, although their democratic stances in relation to their religion did influence not only the radical democratic movements of the United Kingdoms but also the constitution of the United States of America.

No one much bothered about how names of places and individuals were spelt until Samuel Johnson and others gave us dictionaries, which led to a general standardisation of spelling and, although I do object to the ever-proceeding Anglicisation of place names, I have mostly made the spellings consistent with the usage on today's Ordnance Survey maps.

In writing this informal story of these murders I have drawn on my researches for my now out-of-print *Illustrious Fife*, and I am grateful to all the writers whose works I read at that time and which are listed in the bibliography of that 1998 book. The bibliography of this book lists only works that are specific to it. My thanks to all those who spoke to me on my travels through Fife and who shared their knowledge of this diverse county with me. My thanks to the staff of Kirkcaldy Central Library for advice. My thanks to my wife, as so often before, for advice and help with proofreading. All errors, where I may have been "word blind" with regard to names and dates, are mine. My thanks to Mrs Alison Kelly for some of the earlier photographs. Alexander Scott's poem "Scotch Religion" is from his *The Collected Poem of Alexander Scott,* 1994. Every effort has been made to trace, contact and elicit a response from copyright holders, and where this has proved unsuccessful, and the work has been reproduced in this booklet, it is with apologies and in the hope that such use in this work will be welcomed.

DUNCAN GLEN, *Kirkcaldy*, 2002

Fanatics have their dreams, wherewith they weave
A paradise for a sect; the savage, too,
From forth the loftiest fashion of his sleep
Guesses at heaven
      From *The Fall of Hyperion*, John Keats.

There is no sure foundation set in blood
No certain life achieved by others' death
      From *King John*, William Shakespeare.

Scotch Religion
Damn
Aa
      From "Scotched", Alexander Scott.

The dead are not dead, their place knows them no more and is ours today. Yet
they were once as real as we, and we shall tomorrow be shadows like them . . .
It is the fact about the past that is poetic; just because it really happened, it
gathers round it all the inscrutable mystery of life and death in time.
      G. M. Trevelyan.

"My own blue Lomonds", Sir David Wilkie.

THE MURDER AT FALKLAND OF
DAVID, DUKE OF ROTHESAY
FROM WEST OF STRATHTYRUM,
VIA ST ANDREWS, TO FALKLAND

Gateway to ruined St Andrews Castle, June 2002.

IN FEBRUARY 1402, on what must have seemed like a day bright with good prospects, the young David Stewart, Duke of Rothesay, the eldest son of King Robert III, rode south from Dundee to visit St Andrews, "in simple fashion and with a moderate following" as Walter Bower put it in his *Scotichronicon* which was composed in Latin in the 1440s whilst its author was abbot of the Augustinian abbey of Inchcolm, the island nearest to Aberdour. It is not clear whether Rothesay, having heard rumours of moves being made against him, was going to St Andrews to take control of the Castle or to use it as a safe haven. That he took only a "moderate following" with him suggests that he was confident that he would be welcomed by the keeper of the castle.

It could be that this confident and unprepared group crossed the river Tay by "The Ferry of the Loaf" as MacDuff, Thane of Fife, is said to have done in one of the mythical stories that have been created around Macbeth, King of Scots. The Eden, with the many marshy acres of the Howe undrained, was then a broad and deep river and the Prince and his followers would have had to swim their horses across at, or near, today's Guardbridge. We know that they then rode eastwards towards St Andrews past the Castle of Nydie which stood on Strathkinness moor some two miles west of Strathtyrum. Today many associate Strathtyrum with a golf course or the more exclusive Strathtyrum House which has associations with Archbishop James Sharp, who bought the estate in 1699, and more recently, the Cheape family who were also at Rossie in the Howe of Fife. With the semi-circular Roman Doric portico on the pedimented centre of Georgian Strathtyrum House we have moved some way from the cruel world that the Duke of Rothesay knew in 1402.

The few minutes that it took him to ride these few miles beyond Nydie were the last in which the man who expected to become King of Scots, and who in 1398 had been elevated as one of the first two Scottish dukes, enjoyed freedom. The other new duke was the young prince's uncle, the Earl of Fife who became Robert, Duke of Albany. With King Robert III, who in 1388 had been incapacitated by a kick from a horse, not fit to rule competently, Albany and Rothesay were rivals for kingly power. It may have been daytime when Rothesay was ambushed between Nydie and Strathtyrum, but it suits my imagination to have this kidnapping happen just as night was falling, with the wind easing as the sun went down over the Eden estuary and the black castle of St Andrews.

The young captive was rushed to St Andrews Castle where his uncle, Albany, had placed a considerable number of his supporters. Tradition has it that Rothesay was lowered into the dreaded black and smoothed-walled Bottle Dungeon in the Sea Tower. It is difficult to imagine how a young and indulged prince of the Kingdom, who was fond of unruly games and trivial sports and had known only the luxuries of his time, would have reacted when he was taken into that Tower and held whilst the trapdoor in the floor of the east room was opened to reveal the darkness of the seemingly bottomless dungeon cut into the bedrock that rises from the sea.

Portico of Strathtyrum House.
The entrance to the Bottle Dungeon,
St Andrews Castle, June 2002.

Albany was notified that Rothesay had been taken and he and the Earl of Douglas, Rothesay's brother-in-law, rode quickly to St Andrews. They may have previously met at Culross, and planned not only to take Rothesay but to seal his dreadful fate. In 1399 Rothesay had replaced Albany when he became lieutenant of the kingdom, even if that was limited to a fixed three-year term of office which could be renewed only by a special council. The efficient and ambitious brother of King Robert III must have seen that appointment of a previously irresponsible young man as the end of his career as King of Scots in all but name.

From the start the conspirators may have regarded St Andrews Castle as only a temporary prison for Rothesay, seeing the secluded Tower of Falkland as a safer place to murder by starvation the high-profile heir to the Crown.

When Rothesay left St Andrews Castle, tradition has it that it was with Albany and Douglas at the head of the small group that formed his escort. Either side of the captive were two knights: Sir William Lindsay of Rossie, a brother of David, Earl of Crawford, who took his style from Rossie in Collessie parish; and Sir John Ramornie whose lands lay in neighbouring Kettle parish. The conspirators could not be many, as too large a force would have attracted attention, even if the figure in their midst was dressed in a coarse brown cloak – or as Walter Bower put it in his *Scotichronicon*, "mounted on a mule and dressed in a rustic tunic". Who could know that the hunched figure was David Stewart, Duke of Rothesay, Earl of Carrick and Prince of Scotland?

Ruined Sea Tower, St Andrews Castle, June 2002. The entrance to the Bottle Dungeon is to the right of the doorway at ground level.

Falkland Palace, with gardens and slopes of East Lomond Hill, in June 2002.

We know that, as the young captive was brought over the moat and through the dark streets of St Andrews, a gale was blowing and heavy rain was driving into the faces of the horsemen. It is very difficult for us to envisage the landscape between St Andrews and the old Tower of Falkland as it was on that stormy night in 1402. Indeed we do not even know exactly what that Tower was like; certainly it was nothing like the elegant palace of King James V and Mary, Queen of Scots, that today is fronted by fine trees and enhanced by a garden of sweeping lawns, herbaceous borders and specimen trees from countries unknown to these monarchs.

As for the *road* that these ambitious men rode along, we would not think these narrow and boggy paths worthy of such a name. The bleak and swampy upland moors of Magus, Strathkinness and Ceres were undrained and the land lacked the smoother contours that centuries of cultivation have given to this difficult terrain. Even the black and silent nights of these days are unknown to most of those who now travel on the higher road from Cupar to Kennoway with superb views along the now rich agricultural land of the Howe of Fife to the Lomond Hills, with Kingskettle's Kettle Kirk and the idyllic-looking village of Freuchie reminders of days when Stewart monarchs rode to hunt in the Forest of Falkland. There was to be no banishing of out-of-favour courtiers to Freuchie for David Stewart, Duke of Rothesay.

On that miserable, moonless night Rothesay, as he was crowded in and urged on by Rossie and Ramornie, would see nothing of what was then an area of forest, bogs and the now-drained Rossie loch, but perhaps he lifted his head as they passed the desolate Magus Muir and, thinking of his confinement, looked up to the Craig of Drumcarrow which offered those who built a broch tower there in perhaps the first century AD not only a defensible position but a wide view of the Tay and the Eden, and eastwards towards the surging seas of Fife Ness. If he had known what awaited him, the young man would surely have chosen to take many wounds from steel blades rather than the slow death that was his fate.

If Rothesay knew their destination he would know that they would take the higher ground to avoid the worst of the bogs, as did pilgrims on their way to St Andrews. His rustic cloak would become ever heavier with the driving rain and the squelch of the bog would contrast with the noisy armour and clang of the threatening steel of his captives. Ceres Burn would be crossed before, below Pitscottie, it enters the deep gorge of Dura Den on its way to join the Eden a little above Dairsie Bridge. Someone awake in Struthers Castle, stronghold since King Robert II's time of the Lindsays of Byres, who became Earls of Crawford, might have heard the galloping

The ruined Struthers Castle in the 1890s.

Ruined Lindores Abbey. Photograph June 2002.

horses. Some hundred and fifty years later Robert Lindsay, from his property at Pitscottie, would ride along these same paths. He would climb Tarvit Hill and look over to the well-proportioned walls of Scotstarvit Tower. He would pass through Ceres, and certainly he visited Struthers Castle to hear his kinsman Sir David Lindsay read from his poems, and at Pitscottie he wrote memorable words on the history made on many stormy nights.

Perhaps Rothesay was royally confident that no harm could come to him and was looking forward to arriving at Falkland as, west of Ceres and near Chance Inn, the road to Cupar was crossed. Ahead were the forests of the Howe and Falkland, but that party of evil intent would have remained on a high path as long as possible before curving down along the lower slopes of the East Lomond to the enclosing woods near their destination. When Falkland's Tower came into sight through the mist and beating rain it must, even for a confident heir to a crown, have looked nightmarish under what were fearful and intimidating circumstances.

Bower related that on arriving at Falkland Rothesay was condemned to be "kept in a certain decent small room" where he was "long guarded by John Selkirk and John Wright until after languishing with dysentery or (as some would have it) with hunger he died the evening of the day before Easter, which fell on 26 March, or on the morning of Easter day, and was buried at Lindores."

14

Ruined Lindores Abbey, probably in the late 1940s.

Several writers have allowed their imaginations to take flight on the funeral procession of the Duke of Rothesay from Falkland to Lindores. The comet that was seen all over Europe in February-March 1402 has been enlisted by such writers as one of those "fearful lights that never beacon / Save when Kings or heroes die". On seeing the comet when it first appeared, Rothesay, whilst viewing it from Edinburgh Castle, is said to have mentioned the warnings of astrologers. It was not difficult to add to these stories by imagining a ghostly night-time funeral procession of torchbearers and chanting monks bearing the royal body to Lindores Abbey by the banks of the Tay.

Whether that procession took place on a moonless night or a sunny day, we can only guess at the route. It could have gone from Falkland to Lindores by a direct route via today's Dunshalt, passing Myres Castle to Auchtermuchty and straight through the hills, by Pitcairlie House, to Grange of Lindores, Den of Lindores and on, by the ruined Denmylne Castle, where Sir James Balfour gathered Scottish manuscripts, to the Abbey. Alternatively, the procession could have turned east at

Ruined Lindores Abbey in June 2002.

East gable of roofless St Magridin's (Old Parish) Church, Abdie, near Grange of Lindores;
and carved Pictish Symbol Stone, at the entrance to St Magridin's. Photographs June 2002.

16

Auchtermuchty to pass along the banks of the now-gone Rossie Loch, and through Weddersbie Wood, said to be haunted, and so to Grange of Lindores. Both these routes would avoid Collessie, although today the B937 through the hills and along Lindores Loch to Den of Lindores has many attractions.

Half way between Collessie and Lindores Loch a minor road branches to pass the small Black Loch and Berryhill and it could be that Rothesay's body was taken along that road. This could be because it was taken first to St Magridin's (Old Parish) Church near Lindores Loch. It is possible that even a Prince, if not being buried in his Parish Church, had first to be taken to the Parish Church nearest the place of burial. Even if this is unlikely, the emotive roofless remains of St Magridin's Church are well worth a visit. The Church was consecrated by Bishop David de Bernham in 1242 and there is good thirteenth-century work at its east end. The birdcage bellcote on the west gable is late seventeenth century and the building was repaired in 1803, abandoned in 1827 and, as an inscription informs, "Repaired 1856, DW". Here also, close to the entrance to the kirkyard, is a Gig House which today shelters a very interesting pre-Christian Symbol Stone which once stood on a low hill overlooking the village of Lindores. This Stone is incised with abstract symbols that have meanings that we can only make guesses about, although a map-maker's bench mark is all too evident, as are marks made recently when this stone was used as a sundial.

Roofless St Magridin's (Old Parish) Church, Abdie, near Grange of Lindores. Photograph June 2002.

At Lindores Abbey, Rothesay's body found "halowit Sepulture" which may have been on the south side of the chancel, close to the High Altar where were buried the infant sons of David, Earl of Huntingdon, who founded this Tironensian monastery about 1190. The ruined fragments of Lindores that still stand are of about 1200 and built of local red sandstone ashlar. Today the ruins stand in a beautifully-tended garden that is part of Abbey Farm.

That Rothesay died of dysentery has been popularly rejected and especially since Sir Walter Scott, in *The Fair Maid of Perth*, allowed his imagination to add lurid details to the unproven history of Rothesay's slow starvation in a dungeon in Falkland Tower. Scott did not go as far as the sixteenth-century historian, Hector Boece, in detailing the gruesome particulars of slow starvation, but even in the less sensational parts of his novel Scott made the most of the early chroniclers' writings that were unfavourable to Albany and Sir John Ramornie. He described not Bower's "decent small room" but a room specially chosen for death by starvation,

> Rothesay's bed chamber in the Tower of Falkland was well adapted for the execution of such a horrible project. A small narrow staircase, scarce known to exist, opened from thence by a trap-door to the subterranean dungeons of the castle through a passage by which the feudal lord was wont to visit, in private, and disguise, the inhabitants of those miserable regions. By this staircase, the villains conveyed the insensible Prince to the lowest dungeon of the Castle, so deep in the bowels of the earth that no cries or groans, it was supposed, could possibly be heard, while the strength of its door and fastenings must for a long time have defied force, even if entrance could have been discovered. Bonthron, who had been saved from the gallows for the purpose, was the willing agent of Ramornie's unparalleled cruelty to his misled and betrayed patron.

That an official enquiry was held into Rothesay's death suggests that some important men were suspicious but, as is the way with governmental enquiries into governmental actions, Albany was found innocent and it was

Gateway to ruined Lindores Abbey, possibly towards the end of the nineteenth century.

Gateway to ruined Lindores Abbey in June 2002.

officially stated that Rothesay had died "through the divine dispensation and not otherwise". No doubt suspicious minds noted that in 1402 Malcolm Drummond, Rothesay's uncle, died in prison in circumstances that echoed Rothesay's end. There was something of a fashion at that time for accusations of assassination by starvation; in England the Lancastrian Party were accused of having disposed of Richard II by this means.

It could be that Rothesay was arrested on a warrant obtained from the King, who was under pressure from Albany and Lindsay, but that is secondary to what happened at Falkland. In his *Original Chronicle*, written in Scots verse, Andrew of Wyntoun does not even hint at murder, but he was writing whilst Albany was still alive. In his *Historia Majoris Britianne* John Mair (or Major) only hinted at murder and Walter Bower, who admired Albany, can be read as almost scorning the idea. Hector Boece (or Boyce), whose history of 1526 was translated into Scots by John Bellenden, 1536, not only embellished the process of starvation with novelettish incidents but added accounts of how miracles were performed by Rothesay's spirit which only stopped when his death was avenged by King James I.

What most modern historians are agreed on is that it was strange to have Rothesay buried, without any grand ceremony, at Lindores rather than at Dunfermline beside other royal personages, including his mother, Queen Annabel, a Drummond who died peacefully in 1401. The funeral expenses were shown in the customs accounts of Perth as £2.1.4. Also we know that within two months of Rothesay's kidnapping Albany was the unchallengeable ruler of Scotland.

The Bass Rock (left) a distant dot on the Forth as seen from the Fife shore, with Berwick Law almost hidden by an oil tanker, 2001.

In 1406, from Rothesay Castle on Bute, the usually ineffectual King Robert III arranged for the new heir to the throne, James, to go to France, officially to be educated but probably to be safe from those who had kidnapped and overseen the death of his brother. These plans, however, went wrong; the Prince had to wait for a month, in winter, on the Bass Rock, which has been described as Scotland's Alcatraz for Covenanting ministers, and when he did sail for France it was in a Danzig vessel with a cargo of hides and wool. Worse followed as, on 14th March 1406, the ship was boarded by English pirates off Flamborough Head and James was to spend the next eighteen years in captivity. The King died within three weeks of his son's capture and the exiled boy became James I, King of Scots. Albany was restored as lieutenant-general and remained in power until his death in 1420.

Walter Bower was hard on Rothesay in his *Scotichronicon*, seeing him, on the death of his mother, returning to his earlier wanton ways. He reported that the King wrote to Albany that Rothesay should be "put into custody for a time until, after punishment by the rod of discipline, he should know himself better."

It has been suggested that the reason why Sir William Lindsay of Rossie, a brother of David, Earl of Crawford, plotted against Rothesay was that the young Prince had jilted Lindsay's sister, Euphemia, in favour of Elizabeth, a daughter of the Earl of March. Rothesay escaped from that marriage to marry Mary (or Marjorie), a daughter of the third Earl of Douglas.

In casting Sir John Ramornie in the role of one of the villains, Sir Walter Scott took aspects of Ramornie's career as described by early chroniclers; they saw him as the close and evil associate of Rothesay, tempting the young man into riotous excesses and suggesting to the Prince that his uncle, the Duke of Albany, could be conveniently murdered. When Rothesay was horrified by this suggestion the knight took against him and from then on plotted his, rather than Albany's, overthrow. The dramatic death with which Scott ended Ramornie's career is certainly purely fictitious, as is the arrival of the Earl of Douglas, too late to save Rothesay but able to deal with the murderers.

It has been suggested that the young Rothesay met Ramornie, or Sir John de Ramorgny as he is recorded as proprietor of the lands of Ramornie, whilst travelling in continental Europe and brought him to the Scottish court. We know, from *The Exchequer Rolls of Scotland*, that Ramornie, who died in 1402, was active in the royal service from at least 1393, several times going abroad as an envoy, and that he was Rothesay's chamberlain and served as a member of the council set up to work with Rothesay when he was lieutenant of Scotland. A sign on the A914 near Pitlessie still indicates Ramornie Mill, with the old Ramornie property lying nearer Ladybank.

The blame for overseeing the murder of Rothesay has been allocated not to men with knightly swords but to the very shadowy John Selkirk and John

East Lomond, as seen from near Ladybank.

Wright who, Bower says, "long guarded" Rothesay in Falkland Tower. Selkirk could be the unidentified man who received fees in the royal service in the 1380s. The burgh accounts show "John Wricht of Falkland" to have been custumar of Kinghorn from 1411 to 1420 and perhaps earlier. He has also been described as "Constable of Falkland". For a time Wright owned a portion of Burnturk which, like Ramornie, is in Kettle Parish and is off the A914 between Balmalcolm and Ramornie Mill. John Wright was convicted of treason and this is usually regarded as belated action by King James I against one of those involved in his brother's death.

At the top of Kettlehill is the hamlet Coaltown of Burnturk and, who knows, Rothesay may have been taken near what is today a delightful spot above the Howe of Fife. Almost unbelievably in 2002, there is a bus that runs, admittedly not every day, from Cupar to Craigrothie, Chance Inn, Cults, then down to the Cupar road to pass near Kirkton of Cults Church where the young David Wilkie sat on many Sundays, perhaps dreaming of what he described as "my own blue Lomonds". Ahead is Pitlessie, where houses made famous in Wilkie's "Pitlessie Fair" can still be seen, and Ramornie, Burnturk, and Balmalcom before the bus turns up Kettle Hill to Coaltown of Burnturk, Rameldry, the farm houses of Ballinkirk and Carriston, the village of Star and the old burgh of once-Pictish Markinch with its magnificent church tower, to the bus station at new town Glenrothes; a journey of some forty minutes, which is undoubtedly quicker than it would have been for the doomed David Stewart, Duke of Rothesay, on a mule and dressed in rustic clothing.

St Drostan's Parish Church, Markinch, June 2002.

THE MURDER AT ST ANDREWS OF CARDINAL DAVID BEATON

FROM BALLINBREICH TO ST ANDREWS CASTLE

The much-ruined Ballinbreich Castle, of the Leslies, stands some 3 km east of Newburgh on the coast road, past the ruins of Lindores Abbey. This drawing was made in the 1920s.

I T IS LIKELY that when Norman Leslie, son of the Earl of Rothes, rode out on Friday 28th May 1546 to take a leading role in the murder of Cardinal David Beaton in St Andrews Castle he did so from the old Leslie stronghold of Ballinbreich, on the Tay east of Newburgh. He may have been joined for part of the way on that solemn journey to St Andrews by his brother William and by John Leslie of Parkhill, also by the Tay and near the ruins of Lindores Abbey where David, Duke of Rothesay's emaciated body was buried in 1402. Another man from near Ballinbreich who travelled to join Leslie in St Andrews was Peter Carmichael of Balmeadow.

John Leslie, kinsman of the Earl of Rothes, was foremost amongst those who wished to see Cardinal David Beaton assassinated. Beaton, who was not a coward, knew of these plotters but, busily strengthening his castle in St Andrews, he was confident that he could deal with them. A meeting in Falkland of important men in Fife was arranged for the first Monday in June 1546. According to John Knox, this was a trap set by Beaton and those he intended to have captured at Falkland included: John Leslie of Parkhill; Norman Leslie, Sheriff of Fife and heir to his father, the Earl of Rothes; Sir James Learmonth of Dairsie and Provost of St Andrews; Sir John Melville, described by Knox as "the faithful Laird of Raith", an estate which is now part of Kirkcaldy; and James Kirkcaldy and William

Kirkcaldy of Grange. Sir James Kirkcaldy's Grange estate was between Kirkcaldy and Kinghorn, and later his family owned the grander Halyards Castle near Auchtertool which has been reduced to a few fragments of the walls that housed King James V on his way to die at Falkland following his defeat at Solway Moss in 1542.

On Friday 25th May 1546 the Leslies did not enter St Andrews together; William Kirkcaldy of Grange, the younger, was already waiting in the town when Norman Leslie came late at night, and John Leslie, who was most suspected of plotting the Cardinal's death, came into the town last. What was decided that night is not recorded but early on Saturday morning, perhaps about 5 a.m., they met in groups in the kirkyard, near the castle.

They watched and waited until the castle gates were open and the drawbridge down; lime and stones were being taken in for the work being done on the castle's foundations. William Kirkcaldy of Grange, with six others, approached the porter. Kirkcaldy asked if the lord bishop was awake and was told, "no". Beaton had been working on his accounts with Marion Ogilvie, his mistress, who had been seen leaving by the privy postern that morning. There had been no movement from that time, with the Cardinal asleep.

Graveyard of ruined St Andrews Cathedral with St Rule's Tower, June 2002.

Whilst Kirkcaldy was holding the attention of the porter and the others with him looked at the work being done and drew the attention of the workmen, Norman Leslie and a few others slipped into the castle. When they reached the middle of the passage John Leslie, with four others, rushed towards the porter who tried to draw the bridge. The porter was knocked down, his head "broken", and the keys taken from him before he was thrown into the fosse. So, as easily as that, the castle was taken. An alarm was raised which alerted the workmen, more than one hundred, to rush from the walls but they avoided a fight and, unhurt, were pushed out through the gate.

The young William Kirkcaldy stood guard at the privy postern to prevent the Cardinal escaping. The others rushed to the "gentlemen's quarters" who also offered no resistance and, unharmed, more than fifty of them were pushed out through the gate. This was achieved by no more than sixteen men, perhaps even as few as twelve.

The disturbance had wakened the Cardinal who asked from his window what was causing the noise. He was told that Norman Leslie had taken the castle. Running to the postern, he saw that the passage was guarded by William Kirkcaldy and returned quickly to his room. Taking his two-handed sword he ordered his young servant to push chests and other pieces of furniture against the door. John Leslie approached and ordered the Cardinal to open the door. Beaton asked, "Who calls?" and was answered, "My name is Leslie". "Is that Norman?" "Nay, my name is John". The Cardinal said, "I will have Norman, for he is my friend." He was told to be content with those that were there as "For other shall ye get none."

Gateway to St Andrews Castle. Photograph June 2002.

Ruins of Blackfriars Chapel, South Street, St Andrews, June 2002.

With John Leslie were James Melville of Carnbee and Peter Carmichael of Balmeadow and they tried to force the door. The Cardinal was silent for some time but eventually asked, "Will you save my life?" to which John Leslie replied, "It may be that we will." "No," said the Cardinal. "Swear unto me by God's wounds, and I will open the door." John replied, "If that was said, is unsaid."

The door proved to be very strong and Leslie called for a burning brazier. Hearing this, the Cardinal, or his servant, opened the door. Beaton backed away to sit in a chair and cried, "I am a priest: I am a priest: ye will not slay me." John Leslie, as he had previously resolved, struck first and Peter Carmichael followed by striking once or twice. James Melville, however, reputedly a "quieter and gentler man", seeing his companions raging, pulled them back and said, "This work and judgment of God (although it be secret) ought to be done with greater gravity." Presenting to the Cardinal the point of his sword he said, "Repent thee of thy former wicked life, but especially of the shedding of the blood of that notable instrument of God, Master George Wishart, which albeit the flame of fire consumed before men, yet cries it a vengeance upon thee, and we from God are sent to revenge it: For here, before my God, I protest, that neither the hetterent [hatred] of thy person, the love of thy riches, nor the fear of any trouble that could have been done to me in particular, moved, nor moves me to strike thee; but only because thou hast been, and remain, an obstinate enemy against Christ Jesus and his holy Evangel." And so the "gentler" Melville struck him twice or thrice with a thrusting sword. The Cardinal died saying nothing but, "I am a priest, I am a priest: fy, fy: all is gone."

26

In the town, word had spread of the attack on the castle and the Provost, Sir James Learmonth of Dairsie, with some three hundred men, came to the side of the fosse to ask what had been done to the Cardinal. Norman Leslie answered quietly that it was best if they went home as the man they called Cardinal had received his just reward and would cause no more trouble. The crowd responded angrily, saying that they would not leave until they saw the Cardinal. And so, in the words of John Knox, Cardinal David Beaton,

> was brought to the east blockhouse head, and shown dead over the wall to the faithless multitude, which would not believe before it saw. How miserably lay David Beaton, careful Cardinal. And so they departed without *Requiem æternam*, and *Requiescat in pace*, song for his soule. Now, because the weather was hot (for it was in May, as ye have heard), and his funeral could not suddenly be prepared, it was thought best, to keep him from stinking, to give him great salt enough, a cope of lead, and a nuke in the bottom of the Sea-touer (a place where many of God's children had been empreasoned before) to await what exequies his brethren the Bishops would prepare for him.

The national view is that Cardinal Beaton was buried in the ground behind the remnant of the Blackfriars Chapel in South Street, St Andrews, but there are those in Fife who believe that his body was taken from the bottle dungeon of the Sea Tower of St Andrews Castle and buried in the Beaton family vault in the kirkyard of Kilrenny. Below Kilrenny is Cellardyke, where once the harbour was known as Skinfasthaven and there were steps which Cardinal Beaton climbed when leaving his Chancellor's barge. Perhaps even a Cardinal of the sixteenth century could appreciate the outline of May Island as seen from the high-standing kirkyard of Kilrenny where now the arms of the Beaton family are crumbling into dust within the walls of their burial enclosure. The Aberdeen Breviary informed that St Adrian was murdered at the monastery on the Isle of May in 874 by Danes and that 6,000 (no less!) martyrs shared the same fate as Adrian.

Isle of May, 2001. An early lighthouse was erected in 1635 by Alexander Cunninghame of the Barns.

Patrick Learmonth of Dairsie, and Provost of St Andrews, owned the island in 1549, as did Andrew Balfour of Mountquhanie in the 1550s, but when Beaton died it may still have been Crown property.

On hearing of Beaton's murder, John Knox rushed to St Andrews to join the Reformers who had taken the castle, but they held it for only fourteen months before it was taken by a French force. After the fall of St Andrews Castle to the French, the men and women of St Andrews chanted,

> Priests content ye noo, priests content ye noo
> For Norman and his company hae filled the galleys fou.

The rebels were lucky to be taken by the French and not the Scottish besiegers who would almost certainly have had them burned at the stake. It was John Knox, not Norman Leslie, who was pressed into service as a galley slave. Remorse has been said to have eaten into the heart of Leslie for his part in the murder of Beaton, but whether he could have expiated that in the battlefields of France, where he died, is another question again.

St Andrews as seen by John Slezer in the late seventeenth century and view of St Andrews from the south-east in 2001.

George Wishart (1513-46) and Patrick Hamilton (1504-28).

When King James V died in Falkland on 14th December 1542 he had been given the news that a daughter had been born in Linlithgow and famously said, "It cam wi a lass [Marjorie Bruce] and it will pass wi a lass" which proved to be false. The dead King's policy of an alliance with France was quickly challenged by King Henry VIII of England who saw yet another opportunity to take the Scottish Kingdom, even if it was peacefully through the marriage of his son to the infant monarch, Mary, Queen of Scots. The Catholic and French party, led by the Queen Mother, Mary of Guise, and Cardinal Beaton, attempted a coup; the Cardinal went to prison and Queen Mary was betrothed to the Prince of Wales. Beaton was soon free, and when Henry invaded Scotland he aimed not only to indulge in the usual killing and spoiling but also to join with plotting Scottish Protestants to kidnap the Cardinal. None of this helped the popularity of the pro-English party in Scotland and the assassination of Beaton swung opinion even more against the Protestant Anglophiles. Henry VIII died in January 1547 and by 1550 his Scottish policy was seen to have failed, and when Mary, Queen of Scots, married the Dauphin on 24th April 1558 the Catholic cause was in the ascendant. The brutalities and burnings of heretics by the Beatons, however, had worked for the Protestant cause as the invasions and presumptions of Henry VIII had worked for the Catholic one.

Cardinal Beaton was a repressor who saw Reformation as a threat not only to the teachings of his Church but also to the privileges that came with high office. It has been estimated that he was responsible for the deaths of fourteen protestant martyrs; to John Knox he was a "bloody butcher" and to the scholar George Buchanan "a cruel tyrant".

The first high-profile Scottish protestant martyr was the young and well-educated Lutherian reformer Patrick Hamilton (1504-28) who, in

The tower of St Salvator's as seen from The Scores. Photograph June 2002.

1528, Archbishop James Beaton, uncle of Cardinal David Beaton, had hideously, and incompetently, burnt in front of St Salvator's College where now his initials are set into the cobbles in front of the tower. The Archbishop was advised by John Lindsay that if he wished to burn any more of his opponents he should do so in deep cellars since "the reek of Maister Patrik Hammyltoun has infected as many as it blew on." The martyrdom of Hamilton was, indeed, a spark that further ignited the flame of the Scottish Reformation, but the suppressions continued, as did the burnings.

Although they are now often obscured by a parked car, set into the roadway outside St Andrews Castle are the initials of the reformer George Wishart, referred to by Melville, in facing Cardinal Beaton, as "that notable instrument of God". Wishart's trial, which took place in St Andrews in 1546 before assembled nobles and clerics, revealed the defendant's brilliant mind and eloquence, but Wishart was being tried to be condemned and he died at the stake outside the castle, watched from the castle wall by Beaton and other dignitaries. The murder of the Cardinal in St Andrews Castle quickly followed that execution.

 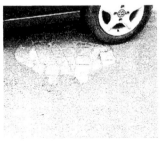

Initials of Patrick Hamilton and George Wishart.

30

The obelisk that is the Martyrs' Monument, which stands alongside The Scores above the eighteenth green of the Old Course and the headquarters of the Royal & Ancient Golf Club, is a reminder of these cruel executions. On its brutalistic pedimented base, with swags and guttae, the letters of the martyrs' names are slowly losing their form as the stone turns to dust. These St Andrews martyrs are: Paul Craw, who was burned at the Mercat Cross where College and Market Streets intersect; Patrick Hamilton; George Wishart; Henry Forrest; and Walter Myln, often been referred to as "the last of the Protestant Martyrs", who was burned at the stake in 1558. The monument was designed (1842-3) by William Nixon who also worked on parts of St Salvator's College.

The massive base of the Martyrs' Monument, St Andrews, in June 2002.

The Martyrs' Monument, St Andrews, June 2002.

SOMETHING OF THE HISTORIES OF
THE FAMILIES INVOLVED IN THE MURDERS OF
CARDINAL DAVID BEATON
AND ARCHBISHOP JAMES SHARP

BEATONS

Cardinal David Beaton was born about 1495 in Balfour House which stood near Markinch between two rivers, the Leven and the Ore, but has been demolished. His parents were John Beaton of Balfour and Elizabeth (or Isobel) Monypenny of Pitmilly near Boarhills. The Monypennys became involved with enemies of the Cardinal and the laird of Pitmilly was involved in the plot to assassinate him. The Earls of Leven at Balgonie Castle were near neighbours of the Beatons of Balfour, as were Balfours at Balbirnie House and the Earls of Rothes at Leslie.

Something of the political strength of the clerical Beatons can be seen in that Cardinal Beaton's cousin Janet, a daughter of David Beaton of Creich near the Tay, was the the second wife of James Hamilton, first Earl of Arran, who was descended, on the female line, from King James II. *Also* Cardinal Beaton's uncle, James Beaton, was Archbishop of Glasgow and of St Andrews, and his nephew, another James Beaton, successfully defeated a placeman of Archbishop John Hamilton to become the last pre-Reformation Archbishop of Glasgow. The ruined Creich Castle stands inland and east of the ruined Ballinbreich Castle, stronghold of the Leslie family, and near the interesting old weaving village of Brunton which, like the old castle and church of Creich, lies in an area encircled by low hills that give expansive views of this region that, twice over, sheltered men who were involved in murder.

The Beaton family were of significance in Fife far beyond these three famous clerics who were powerful secular administrators. Various lines of the family were important landowners around Markinch, Anstruther and Kilconquhar and Beaton's relations married into most of the other land-owning families of Fife including Anstruther, Sandilands of St Monans, Lindsay of the Byres (an Earl of Crawford), and Leslie (a daughter of the Earl of Rothes).

Balfour House, Markinch, now demolished, and ruined Creich Castle, from drawings of the 1890s.

Sir James Kirkcaldy of Grange was favoured by King James V who, in 1540, bestowed on him the castle and barony of Kinghorn and also the lands, tower and fortilice of Grange; about this time Sir James was also given Nether Piteadie and later his son, Sir William Kirkcaldy, was at Halyards in the old parish of Auchtertool. Sir James was regarded by Cardinal Beaton as one of those plotting against him and, following Beaton's murder, he was outlawed in 1546. Kirkcaldy did not regain either Kinghorn or Grange but he survived to die peacefully at Halyards. It was his son, Sir William, who recovered Grange and also Halyards, and his varied career has been told many times.

Following their capture by the French, the rebels who had held St Andrews Castle were taken first to Fécamp and then upriver to Rouen where the prisoners who were seen as nobles were separated from those, including John Knox, who were sent to the French galleys. Sir William Kirkcaldy and his father, with Peter Carmichael, David Monypenny and possibly John, Norman, Robert and William Leslie, were first taken to Cherbourg and then to the more secure and formidable Norman fortress of Mont Saint-Michel. In 1549 Kirkcaldy and Carmichael were amongst those who disarmed their keepers and escaped to England. Losing his pension on the death of King Edward VI of England in 1553 and the accession of the Catholic Mary, Kirkcaldy returned to France to fight for King Henry II. On his return to Scotland he married Margaret, a daughter of Sir James Learmonth of Dairsie, and Provost of St Andrews. Daring deeds followed in Scottish wars. He had a command with Regent Moray's army against Queen Mary at the battle of Langside and showed excellent tactical awareness and leadership. He was rewarded with the governorship of Edinburgh Castle and he used this command when, during the years of Mary's imprisonment in England, he changed sides to hold Edinburgh Castle for the Queen.

MELVILLES

Eight Kirkcaldys and four Melvilles were amongst those involved in the murder of Cardinal Beaton who were named in the Proclamation read at the Mercat Cross of Cupar by John Paterson, Carrick Pursivant. The Carnbee estate of Sir James Melville (or Melvin), who formally addressed

Left: 1890s drawing of ruined Piteadie Castle, north-west of Kinghorn, which dates from the late fifteenth century. Centre: much-restored sixteenth-century Dairsie Castle, photograph April 2002. Right: ruined Dairsie Castle from a drawing of the 1890s.

Cardinal Beaton before striking the final murderous blows, was north of Pittenweem on the east side of Kellie Law. Carnbee is not far from Kellie Castle which was for a long time the Fife property of the Lords Oliphant; later, Erskines, Earls of Kellie, lived in this now well-restored castle. It seems to have been Sir James Melville, nephew of Sir John Melville, who acquired Carnbee about 1309 and members of that branch of the Melvilles were there until 1598. Following the fall of St Andrews Castle, James Melville was, like the others seen as having nobility, imprisoned in a French castle, possibly Brest in his case, and very shortly he "departed from the miseries of this life."

The Sir John Melville referred to in relation to the suppressions of Cardinal Beaton as "the faithful laird of Raith" was the fifth laird of Raith, an estate west of Kirkcaldy. Through the influence of Archbishop Hamilton he was executed on 14th December 1548 aged 46 but, as a somewhat complicated family history shows, his descendants did not suffer from their father's involvement with Beaton's murder. Two of Sir John Melville of Raith's three sons were the courtier and diarist Sir James Melville of Halhill, near Collessie and Monimail, and Sir Robert Melville of Murdocairney, well known through his involvement with Mary, Queen of Scots. He became the first Lord Melville in 1616 and lived to be 93, dying in 1621. His only son, Robert, died in 1635 and the title reverted to the Melvilles of Raith.

In 1643 a very young George, fourth Lord Melville, took Raith into the barony of Melville; in 1690, in the time of William and Mary, he became the first Earl of Melville and was President of the Privy Council. He lived until 1707 and, growing weary of political power, had the very grand Melville House, near Monimail and Collesie, built between 1697 and 1703. Melville's eldest son, Alexander, Lord Raith, had Raith House built 1693-6, but as he died before his father, his brother David became second Earl Melville. In 1713, on the death of his mother, Catherine Leslie, who was Countess of Leven in her own right, being descended from General Alexander Leslie, first Earl of Leven, David Leslie became third Earl of Leven as well as second Earl of Melville. Melvilles were at Melville House into the twentieth century, but in 1725 the Earl of Leven and Melville sold the Raith estate to Robert Ferguson whose family became influential in Kirkcaldy, and there are still Munro-Fergusons at Raith.

Close to Melville House is what is known as Monimail Tower which is what remains of an Episcopal palace. The credit for erecting this palace has been given to Bishop Lamberton (1298-1328) and Cardinal Beaton may

Left to right: Raith House, Melville House and Monimail Tower from drawings of the 1890s.

have repaired it for use as one of his residences. It is certain that Beaton's successor at St Andrews, Archbishop John Hamilton, made Monimail his residence, but it may have been reduced to its current size soon after his death.

If, as seems likely, Cardinal Beaton had Monimail repaired and altered that would be in line with the work he was having done on his castle at St Andrews at the time of his murder. St Andrews Castle was a castle for bishops, but the abolition of Episcopacy in 1560 ended its use as an Episcopal castle or palace and it was well ruined by the late seventeenth century. The reformers who took over the castle following Beaton's murder were besieged by the French and the castle was destroyed by the gunners of a French fleet. Whilst the oldest parts of the castle date from the thirteenth century, much is later than 1547 when Archbishop Hamilton began rebuilding.

LESLIES

Alexander Leslie, first Earl of Leven, who was a veteran in the Swedish service of Gustavus Adolphus, came home to take command of Covenanting armies in the 1640s. His castle was Balgonie, on the River Leven near Markinch, and this early tower-house, which may date from the late fourteenth or early fifteenth century, has been restored in recent years. It faces lands where once stood Balfour House, the birthplace of Cardinal David Beaton. Sir Alexander Leslie also commanded an army that fought Cromwell, but he was old and the real leadership fell to his nephew Sir David Leslie, who became the first Lord Newark in 1661 with his castle at St Monans where he was buried in the old kirkyard. Sir David Leslie is also remembered for his victory over James Graham, Marquis of Montrose, at Philiphaugh, near Selkirk, in 1645 but this Covenanting victory was tainted by the massacre of prisoners.

In 1546 the murderers of Cardinal Beaton were led by Norman Leslie, son of George, third Earl of Rothes. This branch of the Leslie family achieved great power during the reign of King Charles II. The third Earl was tried for the murder of Beaton but acquitted. John Leslie of Parkhill was found guilty but eventually his lands were restored to him. Despite the triumphant Catholic song, Norman Leslie, as the son of the Earl of Rothes, was one of those involved in Beaton's murder who did not go to the slavery of the galleys but to a secure French castle. Like William Kirkcaldy of Grange, Norman Leslie fought for the French and, when dying of wounds received on 31st August 1554 at the battle of Renti, is said to have regretted the part he played in the murder of Cardinal Beaton.

King James II, following his destruction of the powerful Black Douglases in 1455, created between 1457 and 1458 four new earldoms, one of which was Rothes. George Leslie, the first Earl of Rothes, had lands not only in Fife but also in Perth, Aberdeen and Moray, but when these were formed into a single Barony the title given to them was Ballinbreich, the old Leslie stronghold on the Tay. The ruined Ballinbreich stands in the old parish of Flisk and many Leslies lie in its little kirkyard, including, at its centre, Andrew Leslie, fifth Earl of Rothes.

Ballinbreich Castle, from McGibbon & Ross's *The Castellated and Domestic Architecture of Scotland;* engraving of Balgonie Castle on the River Leven; and Leslie House from a drawing of the 1890s.

In later times the Earls of Rothes were associated with Leslie, near Glenrothes and Markinch. Before the Leslie family became the local lairds, the village of Leslie, which became a burgh of barony in 1458, was known as Fettykil, or Fythkill. Additional titles of John Leslie, Earl of Rothes and Duke of Rothes, included Marquis of Ballanbreich, Earl of Leslie and Lord Auchmuty. The "new town" of Glenrothes, which dates from the early 1950s, takes its name from the Earls of Rothes.

Following the execution of Charles I on 30th January 1649, Charles II, now needing Scotland, was in St Andrews on 4th July from where he rode to Falkland via Cupar. Important Fife families had representatives with the King and he visited some of them, including the Earl of Wemyss at Wemyss Castle. He also rode through the Lomonds to dine with John, Earl of Rothes, then just come of age but who had succeeded his father the year before.

Rothes carried the sword at the coronation of King Charles II at Scone in January 1651 and he marched for his King to defeat at Worcester by Cromwell. Rothes went to the Tower of London, as did the Earl of Kellie. Cromwell's troops were soon everywhere in Fife, living off the land and the people. In 1652 the diarist John Lamont noted, "This year the English began to cut downe Falkland Wood; the most part of the trees being oakes." Following his Restoration in 1660, King Charles II did not need Scotland as he had in 1649; Falkland was not visited by him, nor again by any Stewart King, and the Hanoverians probably had not even heard of it.

Charles II ruled Scotland through Commissioners. Rothes was again a man of power who implemented the Acts by which Episcopalianism was restored and all who worshipped as Presbyterians were doing so outside the law. He was made President of the Council and became even more important when John Middleton fell from Royal favour in 1663. The Pentland Rising of 1666, prompted by the methods used by Sir James Turner's troops to suppress illegal church services or conventicles and collect fines from those who attended them, cost Rothes his powerful position as Royal Commissioner to Parliament but, having Royal protection, he was created Lord Chancellor.

The very grand Leslie House, by the River Leven, was built for John Leslie, Earl and Duke of Rothes. It did not survive a hundred years, being destroyed by fire in 1763, and only the west wing was rebuilt. Today Leslie House is a Church of Scotland Eventide home for the elderly. Surprisingly, when newly built, Leslie House could be a safe haven for law-breaking Covenanters. The wife of the great Rothes, Lady Anne Lindsay, a daughter of the Earl of Crawford who had provoked King Charles II by refusing to abjure the Covenant, remained a Presbyterian who, Protestant myth-makers like to believe, may even have attended conventicles. Perhaps Rothes, who was married in his late teens and lived during the first years of his marriage in his father-in-law's castle of Struthers, was not all hard heart as he is reputed to have said to his wife, "My hawks will be out tonight, my lady, so you had better take care of your blackbirds." It does seem that many men of the Howe of Fife, as well as villagers in Falkland, Leslie, Markinch and Kettle owed their liberty to her warnings. There is documentary evidence to show that when the Bishop of Dunkeld deposed all the other non-conforming ministers in his diocese, the Rev Thomas Black of Leslie remained, although in 1663 he had been ordered by the Privy Council to move out; Lady Anne's influence on Rothes was surely crucial.

The body of the Duke of Rothes was brought from Holyrood Palace, via Leith and Burntisland, to be placed, with trumpets sounding and a display of ducal ostentation, in the Leslie vault in Christ's Kirk on the Green. The original building has been replaced, but this is a name that has sounded down the centuries not for great soldiers or noble autocrats but for a wild outdoor party as described in a famous poem – " Christ's Kirk on the Green" which begins, "Was never in Scotland heard nor seen / Sic dancing nor deray".

Although David Hackston of Rathillet enjoyed wild parties in his youth, it is unlikely that he and the other extremist Covenanters would have approved of such goings-on on the green in front of Leslie's Christ's Kirk.

Leslie, with Christ's Kirk on the Green, in the late 1940s before Glenrothes was established as a New Town that has almost surrounded Leslie.

THE MURDER OF ARCHBISHOP SHARP

THE MURDERERS CONSPIRE

ON TUESDAY the eighth of April 1679, as previously arranged, a meeting took place at Alexander Balfour's house in Gilston. This house was near today's Gilston Mains Farm which lies north-west of the late-nineteenth-century Gilston House which stands off the A915 between Upper Largo and Largoward. Amongst the men there were David Hackston of Rathillet (near the village of Kilmany), John Bonner, the younger, of Greigston (in Cameron parish), John Lindsay of Baldastard (west of Gilston), James Ness from Hill Teasses (a neighbour of Baldastard Mains), David Watson from St Andrews, Robert Henderson from Balmerino (north of Rathillet, by the Tay), James Youle from Lathockar (off today's A915 beyond Higham Toll), George Fleming, younger, from Balbuthie (east of Kilconquhar), Alexander Henderson, son to John Henderson from Kilbrackmont (north of Balcarres, the home of the Earl of Crawford and Balcarres above Colinsburgh), John Scott from Lathones (not far from today's Largoward), a Hackston from Nether Largo, and two Balfours, James and George, in addition to Alexander Balfour in whose house the meeting was held.

David Hackston, or Rathillet as he was known after his property, asked why he had been called to the meeting and Robert Henderson and Alexander Balfour explained that they were concerned about the increased persecution by William Carmichael, a Sheriff Clerk who enforced the laws suppressing the Presbyterian Covenanters who would not accept Episcopalianism. Examples were given of those who had been persecuted, including James Mill, a near neighbour of Rathillet in Kilmany.

A Captain Lumsden had sent a sergeant with six soldiers to Kilmany to search for James Mill, with orders that if they missed him to shoot his horse, which they did whilst Mill escaped by the back door and rode on

39

another horse to Rathillet where he met "James Hackston and James Kenneir, his brother's man". They met two others and decided not to run further but rather to return to Kilmany. On reaching the village they burst in on two soldiers in James Mill's house, disarming them. They then went out into the village to deal with other soldiers who were moving between houses. There were no deaths but one wounded soldier, Gilbert Duncan, swore that he would eat nothing until he had his revenge, and for this show of defiance he had his head "broken" again.

The next day Alexander Wilson, ensign to the company, came to Kilmany with 60 soldiers who fired shots to intimidate the villagers. This was answered by shots from the hillside and a woman informed the soldiers that many more guns would soon be on the hills. In truth those that fired on the soldiers were shepherds and the only others on the hills were those who had abandoned the village which they believed was about to be burned to the ground. The soldiers retreated, having advised the villagers to return the King's arms that they had taken from them.

The conspirators meeting in Alexander Balfour's house in Gilston would be encouraged by this story, and also by being told that those particular soldiers who retreated from Kilmany were fined, and so "wanting pay" they "went all sundry, and never met again".

Following the detailing of the events in Kilmany, little more was said at the first meeting of the conspirators as an alarm was sounded, but another meeting was arranged for Friday night, the 11th of April, at John

Kilmany Parish Church, which dates from 1768, in 2002. From 1803 to 1815 Dr Thomas Chalmers was minister at Kilmany which was busy with the crowds that came to hear his evangelical sermons. Today the village has a statute of the late Jim Clark, the racing car driver, who was born in Kilmany.

40

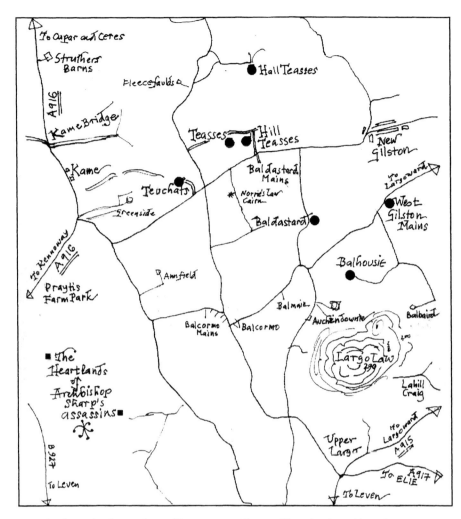

Sketch map showing Teuchats, Hill Teasses, New Gilston, Baldastard Mains, Baldastard, West Gilston Mains, and Balhousie.

Nicholson's house, a collier who lived near Lathones. At that meeting it was decided to take some action against Carmichael "to scar [frighten] him from his cruel courses". There was some debate as to whether this should be done "in his coming or going from St Andrews" or to fall upon him in St Andrews. It was decided to take him in the town and that if he should be in Archbishop Sharp's house to hang both of them over the city port. They decided that this was especially appropriate for the bishop who had "shed and was shedding so much of the blood" of the Covenanters. These men were remembering that in May 1546 Cardinal Beaton's murderers had exhibited his body over the wall of St Andrews Castle.

All this was referred to a meeting to be held in David Walker's house in Leslie on Friday 18th April.

David Walker and James Walker had aroused the hatred of Archbishop James Sharp who urged John Leslie, Earl of Rothes, to have them hanged.

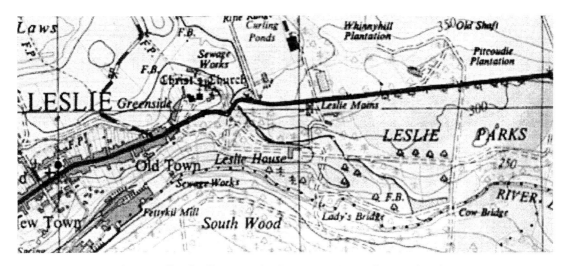

Map of late 1940s showing Leslie and Leslie House on the River Leven. A minor road goes northwards through the Lomond Hills to Falkland. Today Leslie House stands in Glenrothes, a new town of the 1950s.

When Rothes ordered them to come to Leslie House his wife, Lady Anne Lindsay, who had remained faithful to her Presbyterian upbringing, asked their servant to bring them to her after they had been interviewed by the all-powerful Earl. Fearing the worst, she asked them what had been said by Rothes; the unexpected answer was, "Nothing but kindness".

Many illegal open-air conventicles were held in Fife, including many on the secluded slopes of the Lomond Hills which separate Leslie from Falkland, and by 1679 the county was, in effect, occupied by the military. Whether government policy or not, discipline was slack and the violence and extortion inflicted indiscriminately by the soldiers helped to gather support for the cause of the religious radicals. It was in the context of this military lawlessness that lairds and tenant farmers (or their sons) encouraged the formation of armed groups to administer rough justice to those they saw as oppressors of their religious freedoms. Others may view these groups as vigilantes but, as has been said, "it was from the impact of Stewart steel upon the Covenanting flint that our modern freedom of thought and belief was born."

Several new conspirators joined the meeting at David Walker's house in Leslie on Friday 18th April, including James Russell of Kettle, who was to play a significant part in the assassination of Archbishop Sharp; James Mill from Kilmany; John Henderson, servant to Kinkell, possibly near St Andrews, "with his master's commission"; John, George and James Martin from Leslie; William Danziel from Cadham (near Leslie), who was also to be involved in Sharp's assassination; and Alexander Reid from Pitlochie which lies west of Strathmiglo, near Gateside. The meeting decided to take Carmichael not in St Andrews but on the moors west of the town. It was also decided that ten or more men "should be mounted presently with horse and arms", with David Hackston of Rathillet, who was not present that night, chosen to command them.

Although stories of Hackston's life are now rare, for a century after his death his was a name that haunted the dreams of sensitive men and women of northern Fife. We can envisage his black figure riding quietly out from Rathillet into dark and silent seventeenth-century nights to attend the meetings that planned to ambush Carmichael and resulted in the murder of Archbishop Sharp.

During the wild years of his youth it would have taken a discerning person to predict that Hackston would be converted by the field-preachers to a faith that took him into the company of religious extremists whose beliefs led to the bloody murder of the Archbishop at Magus Muir. As a landed gentleman Hackston would have some wealth and influence. His father was laird of Hill Cairnie, which sits below Myrecairnie Hill on the road from Rathillet to Cupar. In 1635 Rathillet became the property of James Hackston of Hill Cairnie and on 3rd March 1670 his son David Hackston was entered as his heir. The heirs of the infamous David retained Rathillet until the end of the eighteenth century, when it was sold by Hellenus Hackston to a Mr Sweet, who sold the property to David Carswell, who in February 1893 sold it to J. D. Harper whose descendants remain at Rathillet. The fine Rathillet House that today stands close to the old farm steading, looking over a formal drive and gardens, was built about 1790.

There is an old two-storied building within the steading of Rathillet Farm that is traditionally believed to be the remains of the farmhouse from which Hackston rode out to attend the meetings of the conspirators and

The building within the steading of Rathillet Farm said to be the remains of David Hackston's property. Photograph April 2002.

from which he set out to join the party that wished to scare Sheriff-Depute Carmichael from his "cruel courses". From that phrase it seems that these extremists were not from the first intent on assassination. Continuing past Rathillet Farm on the road that goes uphill to Mountquhanie (with grand mansion, ruined castle and neat Mains Farm), and standing by the bridge that crosses the burn which passes near Hackston's old house, we can almost believe that we can see what Rathillet was like in 1679.

Mountquhanie mansion was built about 1820 to a design by J. Gillespie Graham. Once this was the property of a line of Balfours who included the Sir Michael Balfour of Mountquhanie who fell with King James IV at the battle of Flodden in 1513. Sir James Balfour of Pittendreich may have lived

Another view of the building within the steading of Rathillet Farm said to be the remains of David Hackston's property, April 2002.

The ruined Mountquhanie Castle, April 2002.

at Mountquhanie as a small boy and for a short time he was certainly
rector of the well-funded Flisk at the time of the Reformation and in 1548
had been with John Knox on a French galley. He married Margaret Balfour
of Burleigh and so became an ancestor of the Lords Balfour of Burleigh,
kinsmen to John Balfour of Kinloch, leader of Archbishop Sharp's
murderers. Balfour of Pittendreich, or Burleigh, enjoyed a career that led
to him being known as "Blak Balfour" and "blasphemous Balfour" and as
"the most corrupt man of his age". He preceded Kirkcaldy of Grange as
Captain of Edinburgh Castle, betrayed Mary, Queen of Scots, and was
suspected of being involved with the Earl of Bothwell in Darnley's murder.

Walking downhill from Mountquhanie to Rathillet on a fine April day in 2002, the view was a peaceful one over a landscape of cultivated lands decorated by the occasional grand house. By the avenue to Rathillet House a pony was sheltering under a large sycamore and uphill the school in the village was silhouetted against a clear but darkening sky.

Rathillet village, with school, towards sunset, April 2002.

Hackston and other conspirators held a meeting on Tuesday 22nd April and on Tuesday 29th there was a meeting in "Millar's house in Magask" which is close to Magus Muir, sometimes known as Magask Muir. At that meeting it was decided that they should "keep Thursday, the first of May, for seeking the Lord's council and assistance". It was also decided that all present should search for John Balfour of Kinloch (near Collessie) and John Henderson, both of whom had "ventured their lives several years before for the gospel".

John Balfour of Kinloch, who was Hackston's brother-in-law, has been named as "John Balfour, or Burley" and some writers have taken this as indicating his family's relationship to Lord Balfour of Burleigh, whilst others, less interested in family histories, have seen it as a description of his physique, small, broad and squat or burly. To a man whom he met in battle Kinloch was "a little man, squint-eyed and of a very fierce aspect". To some of his contemporaries he was seen as "not of the most religious", but, since his minister in Collessie, Reverend John Littlejohn, conformed to the restored Episcopacy, as did his successor John Ogilvie, it is likely that Balfour would be taught by field-preachers at conventicles. John Howie, author of *The Scots Worthies,* described Balfour as having been "always zealous and honest-hearted, courageous in every enterprise, and a brave soldier, seldom any escaping that came into his hands." The Duke of Hamilton knew of Balfour and said that he prayed that "he might never see his face, for if he should, he was sure he would not live long." Balfour was a natural-born soldier, rather as were the great earls of Douglas, including the fourth earl who died at Otterburn and is immortalised in the ballad,

46

My wound is deep; I fain would sleep,
Take thou the vanguard of the three,
And hide me by the braken bush
That grows on yonder lilye lee.

Of course few historians have seen the Covenanting Balfour in the same light as they have the knightly Black Douglases.

It was in 1528 that King James V gave to David Balfour of Burleigh "half the lands of Kinloch, with the Smedylandis, Brewlandis and Cotelandis thereof", together with the right to build a mansion and enclose sufficient policies. The Balfours of Burleigh were prone to lose this property but a later Balfour at Kinloch was a son of Sir James of Pittendreich and Mountquhanie, the devious "Blak Balfour", but his involvement in the murder of Darnley again meant the loss of Kinloch which in 1579 went to John Ruthven, son of William Lord Ruthven. A hundred years later the property achieved a new fame through John Balfour, or "Burley", although he did not know today's Kinloch House which dates from about 1700. The great sixteenth-century stronghold of the Balfours of Burleigh stands, roofless, near Milnathort by the A911.

In 1677 Captain Carstairs was ordered by the Privy Council to seize Balfour but, at Kinloch, Balfour and fifteen others, one of whom was James Russell of Kettle, fired a volley from the house and then pursued the retreating soldiers on horseback, shouting to Carstairs to "yield, and render himself in the name of God and of the Covenant". These Fife lairds were nothing if not brave – or foolhardy! Nevertheless, it was just as well that Hackston did not know what horrors awaited him, as they did also other less-guilty Fife Covenanters including those buried near Magus Muir.

Trees of the Bishop's Wood at Magus Muir with the railed graves of Covenanters just discernible through them, April 2002.

It was Wednesday morning when the meeting that began on Tuesday 29th April broke up and a considerable number of the conspirators went to Bussie and stayed all day where it had been arranged that they meet on Friday night, "for taking some course with Carmichael" on Saturday. They also resolved to prepare a notice reminding those in Cupar of the "robberies and spulzies [plunderings] by James Carnegie and his soldiers, by virtue of an order from that adulterer William Carmichael, held on to by that perjured apostate Prelate Sharp, a known enemy to all godliness" and threatening any who bought any of their poyned [impounded] goods with terrible consequences. That night Rathillet fixed that warning to the school door in Cupar believing that it would "put a great terror to all these persons who were accessory to the present troubles, troopers, soldiers, judges, clerks, and all others in that shire".

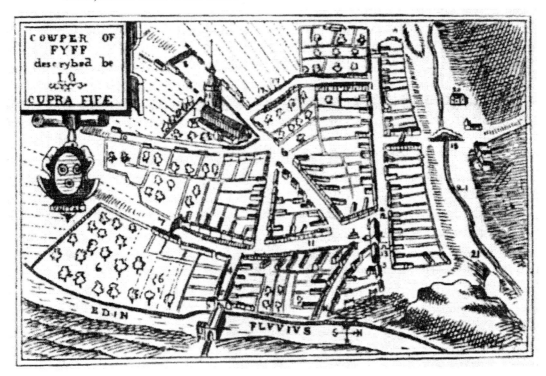

Cupar of Fife, as in Gordon of Rothiemay's map of 1642.

Cupar Parish Church spire,
drawing of the 1890s.

48

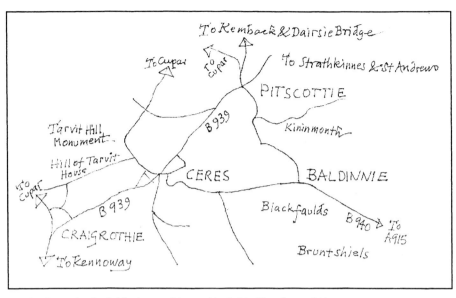

Sketch map showing Baldinnie, east of Ceres, with Blackfaulds and Bruntshiels.

On the night of 2nd May 1679, on the moor, or the Back Wood, near Gilston, the agreed party met but they decided to let one go as they did not trust him with their plans. The others were David Hackston of Rathillet, John Balfour of Kinloch, James Russell from Kettle, George Fleming from Balbuthie, Andrew Henderson, Alexander Henderson from Kilbrackmont, William Danziel from Cadham, James, Alexander and George Balfour from Gilston, Thomas Ness from Hill Teasses, and perhaps Andrew Guillan, weaver in Balmerino and said to be from Falkland, who had been put out of Dundee "for not hearing the curate". There is some doubt as to whether Guillan was there from the start or joined the assassins later.

Lacking information on Carmichael's movements, the twelve horsemen were anxious that, with troopers and soldiers in Cupar, Luderney, Balchristie (near Colinsburgh), Largo and Auchtermuchty, they might be discovered and went, for fear of being arrested, to Robert Black's house in Baldinnie (east of Ceres) although he was away from home. Putting up their horses, praying and sending one of the group to Cupar to learn of Carmichael's whereabouts, they then lay down to sleep in Black's barn.

About 7 o'clock the messenger returned from Cupar with news that Carmichael, on horseback with one other and three on foot, had gone south from Cupar towards Tarvit Hill to enjoy some hunting. Some of the group immediately mounted their horses but others thought it best that Rathillet should go alone to look for Carmichael and give a sign if he found him, when they would join him. This was agreed to and Rathillet rode off down a steep brae, but almost immediately his horse unseated him and whilst dragging his rider down the brae broke his bridle and ran away. The others saw what had happened and sent Alexander Henderson to help Rathillet recapture his horse, but he managed on his own and quickly rode away unhurt.

49

Tarvit Hill. The monument was erected in 1897 to mark the Diamond Jubilee of Queen Victoria.

James Russell, Alex Henderson, George Fleming and George Balfour then saw a horseman whom they took to be Carmichael, but on overtaking him found that it was the Laird of nearby Blebo, who was a Bethune descended, like Cardinal Beaton, from the Bethunes of Balfour. William Danziel having caught up with them, they went west toward Tarvit Hill on the north side, with Rathillet soon joining them with news that he had seen Carmichael go into Cupar and that they could have had him in the fields if they had not dithered about what action to take. The whole day was to turn on such unplanned turns of events.

Turning back along the west side of the hill, and then towards Ceres, they saw two hunters on foot and then two horsemen going into Ceres, but neither of them was Carmichael and they turned eastward where they were met or rejoined by Andrew Guillan who advised them where to go. Throughout that eventful morning there was much "democratic" discussion; in this these men of God's Word were being true to the ideals of their Presbyterianism. Having heard Guillan's advice, John Balfour said that he believed that he was being advised by God, and that he now was convinced that events were about to turn in their favour and they would be successful.

These discussions, or declarations, were interrupted when a boy from Baldinnie approached them to ask, on behalf of Robert Black's wife, how

50

they were progressing. When the men had hidden in Black's barn his wife had blessed them and emphasised that if Alexander Leslie, minister at Ceres, was with Carmichael they should "lay him on the green also". The boy was told to report that they had missed Carmichael. They also asked after James and Alexander Balfour and Thomas Ness who had not re-joined them. The boy said that they were gone but that he was willing to go and ask them about the preaching which they expected to be on the north side tomorrow. The boy left but soon returned with the unexpected news from Black's wife that, although Carmichael had not been seen, the coach of Archbishop James Sharp was approaching. Moving quickly, they saw the coach between Ceres and Blebo. They responded as might be expected saying, "Truly, this is of God, and it seemeth that God hath delivered him into our hands; let us not draw back but pursue; for all looking on it, considering the former circumstances, as a clear call from God to fall upon him."

However, even at this moment when decisions were urgently needed, they continued to "democratically" discuss their position. George Fleming saw nothing to be gained by sparing the Archbishop's life, arguing that if he lived they would be in more danger than if they killed him. James Russell spoke of praying and having more than ordinary outlettings of the spirit for a fortnight together at Leslie, and that his reading of several scripture had convinced him that the Lord would employ him in some service involving a great man who was an enemy of the Kirk of God who would be cut off. William Danziel spoke similarly and so "with one consent" they wished Rathillet to command them to proceed.

Rathillet, however, declined to lead them as it was known that he had a prejudice against the bishop and that this would "mar the glory of the action", for it would be imputed that he sought revenge for being arrested and put in Cupar jail by the Archbishop's chamberlain for a debt that the Hackstons owed to Archbishop Sharp. Nevertheless, he emphasised that he was "willing to venture all he had for the interest of Christ" and would not leave them or hinder them from what "God had called them to". So it is that we can envisage the dark figure of Hackston, seated on his horse with his black cloak muffling his face, watching the terrible deeds of his dismounted compatriots.

On hearing Hackston's words John Balfour said, "Gentlemen, follow me," and all nine of them, taking the easiest route over the small hills, rode as fast as they could to Magus Muir.

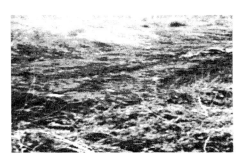

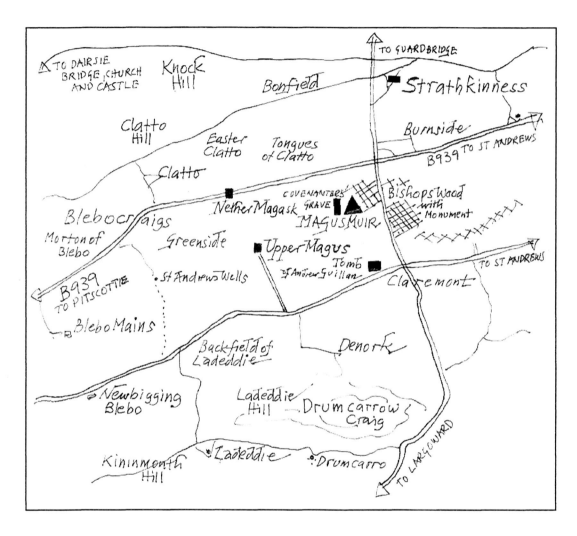

Sketch map showing Magus Muir, near Upper Magask, with the grave of the Covenanters, the monument marking the place where Archbishop James Sharp was murdered, and Claremont with the tomb of Andrew Guillan.

ARCHBISHOP JAMES SHARP

Archbishop James Sharp, engraving after a portrait
by Sir Peter Lely.

JAMES SHARP is a man who has been treated to many harsh
words on his nature and personality as well as on his Episcopal
views; schemer, greedy, devious, are three of the kinder ones. To the
stern puritans of the Covenant Archbishop James Sharp was a Judas; on
his tomb in St Andrews he is a Holy Martyr; to Oliver Cromwell he was Mr
Sharp of that ilk. Cromwell gave that opinion of the smooth-tongued
minister of the kirk following a conference at which Sharp persuaded the
Protector that it was in his interest to favour the Resolutioners or
Moderate Royalist party amongst the Scottish churchmen against the
radical Protesters who would be as ready to oppose Oliver as Charles.

Sharp was imprisoned in London by Cromwell but talked his way to
freedom. Following Cromwell's death, Sharp went to Breda to employ his
courtly style in ingratiating himself with Charles II. Whilst it is to be
expected that Sharp was welcomed by the Episcopalian Royalists as a
fellow-traveller, it is less clear, although a tribute to his diplomatic skills,
why, after the Restoration, his fellow moderate Presbyterians trusted him
to protect the interests of their Church and prevent the King from breaking
the Covenant which he had sworn. None knew better than Sharp how to
use words to conceal his true thoughts. Those sympathetic to Sharp have
maintained that he merely accepted the inevitable. That he moved with the

times, and that, in opposing the violence of the extremists, he gradually accepted, rather than assisted, the restoration of Episcopacy and the Royal supremacy as being the only achievable peaceful settlement in a divided Scotland. Against Sharp, it is clear that even the Episcopal Burnet disliked Sharp as much as did Wodrow, the Presbyterian historian. In the Spring of 1661 Sharp was corresponding with his Presbyterian friends, indignant at the "clandestine whispers" that he was trimming, and "commits himself to his faithful Creator, who will bring his integrity to light." In London, as the representative of the Resolutioners, the sharp Mr Sharp changed sides without informing those whom he represented, and agreed with the influential Clarendon that Episcopacy could be restored in Scotland. His reward for betraying those for whom he spoke in London was elevation to the position of Archbishop of St Andrews.

Like King Charles II, Sharp was revealed as at best a twister of language and at worst a liar. Certainly the moderate Resolutionists were reassured when, in September 1660, their King wrote in a letter to the Presbytery of Edinburgh that "we do also resolve to protect and preserve the government of the Church of Scotland, as it is settled by law, without violation." To David Forrest, minister of Kilconquhar, inland and west of Crail in the East Neuk of Fife, James Sharp was the "greatest knave that ever was in the Kirk of Scotland", which is a very high achievement!

James Sharp, son of William Sharp, Sheriff-clerk of Banffshire, was born in Banff Castle in 1618 and educated at the University of Aberdeen. It was said by Wodrow that Margaret Bruce, the daughter of the minister of Kingsbarns, near Crail, had a narrow escape from becoming Sharp's wife.

Kingsbarns Parish Church of about 1630, altered in 1810-11, and again in 1866 when the top section of the tower and the spire were added. The eye-catching Kingsbarns Primary School dates from 1822 ; the mason was John Cairns and the wright William Bonthron. Photographs June 2002.

She had decided to marry him not least because of a very good sermon, in English, that he had delivered as being his own. The serious and studious Margaret, however, found it printed in a volume in the manse library and the "peccant preacher's" proposal was not accepted as he had been encouraged to expect, but given a briskly delivered rejection.

Sharp married Helen Moncrieff of Randerston, near Kingsbarns. Today the laird's house at Randerston, which may date from the late sixteenth century, stands close to a nineteenth-century farm steading. According to the all-knowing John Lamont (Diary, November 1659) Moncrieff of Randerston's heir was "a lousse liver" and so "ere he depairted out of his life at Randerston" disinherited his son and desponed his estate to his two sons-in-law, "viz. Kingaske, surnamed Ingels, in Cupar, and Mr James Sharpe, minister of Crail" As James Wilkie commented in 1931, "The future Archbishop seldom failed to make the best of both worlds."

Helen Moncrieff and James Sharp's daughter, Isabel, who witnessed her father's murder, married John Cunninghame of the Barns. Their son became Sir William Sharp of Scotscraig, a property by the Tay with a superb view over to St Andrews, which his father bought two years after he became Archbishop. It hardly needs saying that when Archbishop Sharp bought this property the Archbishops of St Andrews were the superiors of Scotscraig. William married Margaret, daughter of Sir Charles Erskine of Cambo.

By 1642 Sharp was a junior academic, a regent at St Andrews University – St Leonard's College. He was probably recommended for the post by Alexander Henderson, a prominent Covenanting minister of Leuchars, who played a significant part in the production of the "National Covenant" of 1638, and by the Earl of Rothes who was then a Covenanter. To get this post Sharp was required to sign the Covenant. It was the Earl of Crawford, patron of the parish of Crail, who in November 1647 presented Sharp to the presbytery of St Andrews to be minister at Crail and, after typically lengthy and searching "trials" Sharp was admitted to Crail in

Scotscraig from a drawing of the 1890s.

1648. The restored King Charles II landed at Dover in May 1660. It was December 1661 when Mr James Sharp, minister of Crail, was consecrated in Westminster Abbey, London, as Archbishop of St Andrews. Times had indeed changed for Scotland, the Scottish people and Kirk!

On 9th January 1662 the Privy Council in Edinburgh restored to the bishops all their old ecclesiastical powers, and banned the meeting of presbyteries and synods without the authority of bishops. An Act of Parliament ordained that no minister who had not been ordained by a bishop could retain his living. To the surprise of the bishops and many leaders of the nation, at least 270 ministers refused to conform and were "outed" from their ministries; many were thrown destitute on the world. Such a minister was required by the Privy Council to settle in a certain parish and failure to do so meant he was "denounced as a rebel, put to the horn, the sheriffs were to apprehend him and put him in prison." The Episcopalians who were given the parishes of the "outed" clergy were contemptuously known to the Covenanters as the "King's Curates".

Crail Parish Church before its restoration,
from an illustration of the 1890s.

Crail's sixteenth-century Tolbooth,
from an illustration of the 1890s.

56

Crail harbour in 2002.

Attendance at Episcopalian services was compulsory and those who failed to do so were harassed, their houses searched and vandalized. These Presbyterians could be heavily fined and kept indefinitely in prison. There are ample records of prosperous lairds being fined £1,000 for attending a conventicle and held in prison for over five years.

The "outed" ministers initially held conventicles indoors, but as the measures imposed by the Government became more drastic these services were held in the open air and usually after dark. A conventicle held in Anstruther in 1668 particularly infuriated Archbishop Sharp, one-time Presbyterian minister of Crail.

Following his London installation as Archbishop of St Andrews in December 1661, Sharp drove north in a coach with three other new bishops – James Hamilton, Andrew Fairfoul (who was born in Anstruther in 1606), and Robert Leighton, Bishop of Dunblane and Archbishop of Glasgow. The least worldly of these four men was Leighton who is said to have refused the title of Lord; he seemingly disliked the ceremony of a public entry into Edinburgh and left his companions at Morpeth. Gilbert Burnet, who refused a bishopric, was a protégé of the "saintly" Archbishop Leighton, and had disagreed with Sharp, witnessed the entry into Edinburgh and later noted, "Though I was thoroughly Episcopal, yet I thought there was somewhat in the pomp that did not look like the humility that becometh their function."

On 15th April 1662 the new Archbishop arrived at the Earl of Rothes' Leslie House to progress in grand style to St Andrews, the seat of

From 1890s drawing of St Mary's Church, Dairsie and Dairsie Bridge over the River Eden.
The bridge carries a panel with the coat of arms of Archbishop James Beaton, c.1530; Archbishop John
Spottiswoode's Church of 1621 had its Episcopal features removed in the 1650s. The exterior, although in theory an
odd mixture of "Gothic survival and innocent classical", makes this rural church a small *tour-de-force,* with the
"hoodmoulded three-light windows, with huge plate-traceried heads" well worth climbing up from the equally well-
built old bridge to see close to. From the A91 there is a choice of three roads, including one in Dairsie village, to this
interesting group of buildings by the Eden.

the Primacy. When Sharp made his staged journey from Leslie to St
Andrews on that sunny Spring morning, the Howe of Fife may have
seemed to him to be heralding a new awakening of the Church as well as of
the wild flowers and the trees that had survived the fellings of the
Cromwellian invaders. Over the Howe from Cupar, down from the moors
by Ceres, along from Dairsie, with its church, castle and old bridge over the
Eden, and through the small hills north of Rathillet and Kilmany rode the
"divers persons and corporations" that the Earl of Rothes had invited.
Round the East Lomond came the Provost and Magistrates of Falkland to
form part of the escort for the man who had undergone a metamorphosis
from plain-clothed minister of Crail to this Archbishop in a grand coach
drawn by six stately horses.

58

As the procession formally set off, Rothes rode on the Archbishop's right hand and Alexander Erskine, third Earl of Kellie, on his left. Like Rothes, Kellie had fought for Charles II in the war against Cromwell, having been at Worcester in 1651, and, after a brief spell in the Tower of London he went into exile in Holland, returning in 1661. In attendance also were David Leslie, Lord Newark, the victor at Philiphaugh, who would have ridden to Leslie from his castle 0.8 km south-west of the old kirk of St Monans, and the twenty-five-year-old Alexander Leslie, the second Earl of Leven, son and namesake of another great general. John Lamont noted in his Diary that there were "estimat to be about 7 or 8 hundred horse" in that procession. The lairds of Rathillet and Kinloch may have glimpsed the massed ranks behind the Archbishop's grand coach, as may James Russell from the heart of the Howe at today's Kettlebridge. Perhaps that unique procession took the same route as that taken sixteen years later by the small party that was halted at Magus Muir. Perhaps the Archbishop sat in the same well-appointed coach from which he was to step down to beg for his life.

In St Andrews, where John Knox, newly returned to Scotland, had preached in the Parish Church, Holy Trinity, on 10th June 1559 against

Kellie Castle in 2001, and 1890s drawing of St Monans Church.

idolatry – "on the cleansing of the Temple" – the Archbishop offended Presbyterian sensibilities by preaching from a velvet cushion, and by diverging from his text, "I determined to know nothing among you save Jesus Christ and Him crucified," to vindicate Episcopacy, the lack of which, he said, had caused the many troubles and disturbances in Church and State. He closed by observing that if the arguments he offered were not convincing, he had "more powerful ones in reserve". This may not have been a satin-gloved threat but the iron glove of military suppression certainly followed.

In his Diary John Lamont said that only two Presbyterian ministers compromised their beliefs by joining the procession that travelled from Leslie House to St Andrews. One was William Barclay, once of Falkland but who had been deposed sixteen years before for supporting Montrose. He was reinstated one year after the great cavalcade to St Andrews and died five years before Sharp was murdered at Magus Muir. Following the overthrow of James VII and the arrival of William and Mary in 1688, at least 200 Episcopalian "King's curates" were driven roughly from their manses as part of the outburst known as the "Rabbling". Like his father, David Barclay, who was minister of Strathmiglo, had compromised with Episcopalianism and was one of those deposed.

Before that Revolution of 1688 much blood was to flow in what Presbyterian historians have seen as "The Killing Times"; years of suffering, sorrow, robbery, imprisonment, banishment, drowning, torture by the "boot", torture by the thumbscrew, martyrdom "by rope and by gun" that continued till only the "'Remnant' and the record remained." On another leaf of that record is the bloody assassination that took place at Magus Muir on 3rd May 1679.

Detail from *The Preaching of John Knox before the Lords of Congregation, 10 June 1559* by Sir David Wilkie. Knox is preaching in St Andrews, having been invited by the Protestant Leadership, the Lords of Congregation, to return to Scotland. Archbishop Hamilton of St Andrews threatened to have his soldiers fire on Knox if he preached but, bravery counting, the rest is history. The idea of a National Covenant, that was signed by all who opposed Catholicism and Episcopalianism, was obviously crucial to the history of Scotland, but so also was Knox's personal courage as a reformer who spoke for freedom and not as a narrow sectarian Calvinist. Wilkie considered painting the murder of Archbishop Sharp, but in the end it was Sir William Allan who produced a Magus Muir painting that was exhibited in London at the Royal Academy in 1821.

ARCHBISHOP JAMES SHARP'S
LAST JOURNEY
FROM EDINBURGH TO MAGUS MUIR VIA KENNOWAY AND CERES

Signing the Covenant in Greyfriars' Churchyard, Edinburgh, in 1638;
detail from an engraving after a painting by George Cattermole.

ON THURSDAY 1st May 1679 James Sharp, Archbishop of St Andrews, Primate of Scotland and one of King Charles II's Privy Councillors was in Edinburgh to attend a meeting of the Council. On the following day he set off by coach for his home in St Andrews. With the Archbishop were his daughter Isabel and six servants.

They went to Leith from where a ferry took them to Kinghorn, to Pettycur Harbour. From there the coach party journeyed along the coast to Kirkcaldy and presumably climbed up the steep path that led past the two towers of King James II's Ravenscraig Castle and thence to Dysart. Above Dysart, and inland from the coastal road through the Wemyss villages to Buckhaven, Methil and Leven, the Standing Stone road cuts through, today as in Sharp's time, to Windygates. This road takes its name from an ancient standing stone, at that time known as the Half-Way Stane. There is something almost Roman about the straightness of the road and it would provide Sharp with some relief from the jolting and bumping and swaying that he would have endured on most other sections of the road from Kinghorn to Ceres. If so inclined, he could look over to the Lomond Hills above Leslie from where, as a newly installed archbishop, he had travelled at the head of a grand procession to St Andrews on 15th April 1662. George Martine of Claremont, Sharp's secretary and companion, kept a Household Book which recorded the expenses incurred by the Archbishop between 1663 and 1666 and from it we learn that Sharp travelled regularly along this road on his way to and from Edinburgh. From these impersonal accounts of the 1660s we learn that William Wallace, who was still with Sharp in May 1679, was already a loyal servant of a much-hated man.

Sharp would know that the River Leven had to be crossed below its confluence with the River Ore. In 1824 John Haig came to this point of the

Leven, at Cameron Bridge, to found his whisky distillery. At Windygates the road to Markinch goes west to pass Milton of Balgonie, the site of Balfour House and the restored Balgonie Castle where Sir Alexander Leslie, first Earl of Leven, once lived, but Sharp's coach continued northwards and uphill to Kennoway. Despite being surrounded by modern industrial structures, the hill on which the Maiden Castle of Kennoway stood remains unmistakable as the village is approached from Windygates. The Maiden has been a contender for the destination of MacDuff, the Thane of Fife, when he fled from Macbeth. The old village of Kennoway may take its name from a St Kenneth of Canlie who established a Culdee Church there in the seventh century. Once a centre of malting and brewing, by the late eighteenth century Kennoway was a village of weavers. Coal miners came from the West of Scotland in the 1930s and also after the Second World War when it was intended to establish a new mining town, but that did not get beyond the drawing boards of town planners and instead we have the New Town of Glenrothes which was planned around a new Rothes colliery. This colliery proved to be a white elephant due to geological problems, although the price of oil and government policy towards the power stations must have influenced the decision to write off Rothes and see Glenrothes as a town with modern light industries.

The old Swan Hotel has seen busier times, but an earlier inn in the Causeway was kept very busy in stagecoach days, as Kennoway was on the main road from Newport and Cupar to Windygates and an important stage on the route to the popular Pettycur ferry. The coaches came along the Causeway, which twists along behind today's main road past the old Church of 1619 which was abandoned in 1849 when a new parish church had been completed. As elsewhere, church builders, farmers and villagers found the church's walls an easy quarry for a new church, barns and kailyard walls, with the enterprisingly creative owner of Drummaird, near

Site of Maiden Castle, Kennoway, June 2002.

62

Dead Wynd, Kennoway, May 2002.

Bonnybank, incorporating the steeple into a now-gone barn. The old Mercat Cross also found a new home but part of it was said to have been rescued.

The Cross stood in the Market Square at the top of the Causeway by the old church and facing it was the Cross House. Although the kirk has gone, its cemetery survives surrounded by a high wall, a section of which runs along Dead Wynd—almost more apt than Anstruther's Burial Brae. Those wishing to see the old churchyard can get the keys from a helpful lady in nearby Forbes House. Near the Cross and Cross House was an inn and it was there that the Archbishop's six sleek horses were stabled and his servants given lodgings. Sharp and his daughter, Isabel, spent the night in Cross House, then owned by Captain Seton who may have been a relative of the Archbishop and who welcomed him several times when he arrived late in Kennoway and did not want to risk taking the rough road over the hills and moors to Ceres and St Andrews.

Photographs of the old seventeenth-century house of Captain Seton have survived and it was famous enough to attract the attention of local historians. In 1906 Andrew S. Cunningham described the house as,

> a seventeenth-century two-storey building, typical of the "town houses" of the Scottish gentry of the period. Gaunt and worn with age, the building is a melancholy link with the past. As one mounts the outside stair, he is assured by the tenant that the west room is "the very room in which the Bishop slept," and attention is called to the wood panelling and the fine old mantlepieces of both apartments. Externally the stringed windows, the crow-stepped gables, and ornate chimney-heads are the only features of the building. A little further down the "Causey" there is another quaint house which is also associated with the name of the Setons, and what gives this old building an air of importance is the fact that a coat of arms is sculpted above the main entrance, the date being 1712. Tradition does not tell us what event in national or local history the stone was placed above the door to commemorate. Writing in May 1793, the Rev. Patrick Wright says, "that a woman died fourteen years ago who remembered to have seen Archbishop Sharp at the manse of Kennoway the day before he was murdered."

Photograph of 1908 showing what is reputed to be the house of Captain Seton, at the head of the Causeway, in Kennoway, where Archbishop Sharp spent his last night. The house has been demolished, although it could be that parts of it were incorporated into a later building.

Captain Seton's old house has gone, but the buildings that replaced it and neighbouring houses make an interesting group. There is Forbes House, Seton House which has a fine central gablet, and also Seath House. Seton House is late eighteenth-century with an 1877 extension. A modern double garage front at Seath House has an old heraldic stone with a date that looks like 1719 and not 1712 as reported by Andrew Cunningham.

In the old kirkyard there is a headstone in memory of Marion Seton and Christopher Seton, Surgeon, who died April 1861, and close to that stone is an interesting, but now unmarked, table memorial stone, which, I like to think, may mark the grave of another Seton. Captain Seton's friends included the Lundin family of Auchtermairnie and in the old kirkyard there is the grave of the last of that important family, Euphemia Lundin who died, unmarried, on 27th February 1855 aged 59.

Heraldic stone on Seith House; headstone of Lundins of Auchtermairnie, in Kennoway old kirkyard, May 2002.

Kennoway old kirkyard, with the stone of Marion and Christopher Seton
fairly upright on the extreme left, May 2002.

Seton House, Kennoway, on wheelie bin day, May 2002,

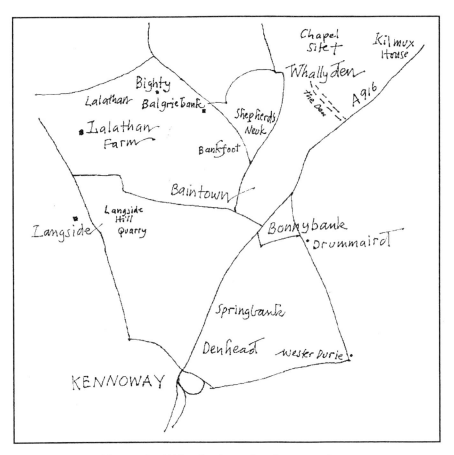

Sketch map of the start of Archbishop Sharp's route from Kennoway to Ceres.

1890s drawing of Scotstarvit Tower.

It was about nine o'clock on Saturday 4th May 1679 when Archbishop Sharp left Captain Seton's house. We can try to envisage the grand equipage drawing away from Cross House, standing gable-end to the Causeway. It must have taken considerable skill to drive the state coach with six horses, coachman, postilion, four servants and two very important passengers along the narrow causey which was cobbled not with today's even-cut setts but with round stones from the burn. If we can only wonder at that grand coach, think what a surprise it would have been to Cardinal David Beaton, who relied on horse and mules for his journeys from St Andrews to his grand barge waiting at Cellardyke to take him across the Forth to Leith from where he rode to Edinburgh and his house in today's Cowgate.

Even with his grand coach and servants the journey from Edinburgh to St Andrews cannot have been one that the Archbishop enjoyed. Today even the higher lands east of Ceres are drained, hedged, fenced and well cultivated but then that area was mostly wild moorland. The route taken by Sharp to Ceres is not easy to identify. Initially the old road may have taken the same line as today's A916 as far as Bonnybank. Above that hamlet lies Baintown and an old track, with right of way, passes Balgriebank and near the ruined Bighty farm which had claims to having the highest hearth in Fife, higher perhaps than the highest farm on the slopes of Largo Law. The view down to Largo Bay and round to Ruddons Point near Earlsferry and Elie is expansive. A short walk to Porter's Brae gives a splendid view of the fields of Carriston, Ballinkirk and round towards Coaltown of Burnturk and the long sweep of the Howe of Fife. To the north-east are the hilly acres that were crossed by the Archbishop's coach. From Bonnybank the old road to Ceres and Cupar that the Archbishop's coach bumped and swayed along probably twisted and turned somewhat west of today's A916. It could have gone from Baintown to Balgriebank and it certainly went to Whallyden, an unusual name that may be a corruption of the Hallow or Halie Den but neither this nor the Chapel that once stood west of Kilmux House may have interested Sharp whose mind might have been on the threats that had been made to his life.

Ahead is Montrave and Clatto Den, east of Clatto Castle, a stronghold of the Setons with Clatto Hill rising to 814 feet and Drumtrissel rising above Clatto Den. Eastwards the greater height of Largo Law rises above the farms where those who conspired against Sharp and his agent, Carmichael, had met—Baldastard, Gilston, and Hill Teasses. Some of these men were already, as Sharp passed through Clatto Den, out on the moors near Ceres. It was, perhaps, near Little Muirhead that Sharp's coach crossed the road that today goes from near Kame Bridge to Paradise Farm and Cults above Pitlessie. The road to Ceres, however, probably cut across to near Struthers Castle where the old road has survived to become part of today's A916, Kennoway to Cupar. A few hours later some of the fleeing murderers may have passed this way before turning north to cross the Eden at Pitlessie.

Today, as the road bends above Chance Inn, the top of East Lomond can be briefly glimpsed as, ahead, can Scotstarvit Tower. From Craigrothie the

Looking over the village green to Ceres Kirk with the Bannockburn Monument, which faces the old bridge and carries the inscription, "To commemorate the indication of Scotland's Independence on the field of Bannockburn 24th June 1314—and to perpetuate the tradition of the part taken therein by the men of Ceres." Photograph May 2002.

Lindsay burial house in Ceres kirkyard, with the separate Parish Church behind it. Photograph, May 2002.

Bishop's Bridge, Ceres, May 2002.

monument on Tarvit Hill can be seen standing high above the trees that hide Hill of Tarvit House, and ahead is Ceres with the spire of the kirk topping the trees that edge what has been described as the "most attractive village in Scotland" with the village green a central feature near the seventeenth-century Bishop's Bridge with Bishop Cottage on the other side. In 1679, as today, Ceres is another world from the old town of Edinburgh.

If the coachman had to take care coming along the Causeway in Kennoway so also, as he approached the old bridge over the burn at Ceres, he must have carefully assessed its width and what line to take to cross it. The coachman's destination was the home of Alexander Leslie, popularly known as "Lang Sandy Leslie", the Episcopal incumbent of the Parish Church. This is the man that Mrs Black of Baldinnie suggested should be treated as she thought Carmichael deserved—"lay him on the ground also". That did not happen and Leslie, who came to Ceres in 1667, left in 1679 to become, like Sharp before him, minister of Crail. He was turned out of his Crail ministry for refusing to pray for their Majesties William and Mary but his memorial stone was erected in Crail kirkyard.

Tradition has it that Sharp smoked his last pipe at Ceres with Alexander Leslie before setting off on the last stage of his journey to St Andrews. Sharp knew of threats to his life and he may have been aware that crossing the moors beyond Ceres was potentially dangerous. He obviously did not, however, consider the number of servants with him as important as he sent one of them to pay his respects to the Earl of

Crawford. In Ceres kirkyard is the burial chamber of the Lindsays which now has a Victorian tomb of John Lindsay, Earl of Crawford, who died in 1749. The Lindsay vault is now detached but was probably once attached, in the late sixteenth century, to an earlier church.

At Ceres Archbishop Sharp was not much more than halfway from Kennoway to St Andrews and ahead of him lay the route, in reverse, that the Duke of Rothesay may have been taken on his way to his imprisonment and death in Falkland Tower. The road may have been straight enough to Pitscottie but the country was rising to the moors beyond Blebo Craigs.

This hurrying party may have been aware of shadows cast by Drumcarrow Craig but, unlike the captive Duke of Rothesay who was forced to travel at night and into driving rain, when Archbishop Sharp reached the village of Magus it was near enough noon on a bright day, and despite the gloomy atmosphere that many visitors have said they sensed at Magus Muir, in fact it was probably a pleasant enough scene until the coachman saw men riding fast towards them. A pleasant landscape on a sunny May day but suddenly a dangerous place to be even with a coach pulled by six rested and fed horses.

View from Ceres eastwards towards Magus Muir. Photograph May 2002.

AN ACCOUNT OF
THE MURDER OF
ARCHBISHOP SHARP
WRITTEN BY
JAMES RUSSELL
WHO WAS ONE OF THE MURDERERS

. . . John Balfour said follow me:

. . . whereupon all the nine rode what they could to Magus Muir, the hills at the nearest, and Andrew Henderson riding afore, being best mounted, and saw them when he was on the top of the hill, and all the rest came up and rode very hard, for the coach was driving hard; and being come near Magus, George Fleming and James Russell riding into the village, and James asked at the goodman if that was the bishop's coach? He fearing, did not tell, but one of his servants, a woman, came running to him and said it was the coach, and she seemed to be overjoyed; and James riding towards the coach, to be sure, seeing the bishop looking out at the door, cast away his cloak and cried, Judas be taken! The bishop cried to the coachman to drive; he firing at him, crying to the rest to come up, and the rest throwing away their cloaks except Rathillet, fired into the coach driving very fast about half a mile, in which time they fired several shots in at all parts of the coach, and Alexander Henderson seeing one Wallace having a cocked carrabine going to fire, gript him in the neck, and threw him down and pulled it out of his hand. Andrew Henderson outran the coach, and stroke the horse in the face with his sword ; and James Russell coming to the postilion, commanded him to stand, which he refusing, he stroke him on the face and cut down the side of his shine, and striking at the horse next brake his sword, and gripping the ringeses of the foremost horse in the farthest side: George Fleming fired a pistol in at the north side of the coach beneath his left arm, and saw his daughter dight [prepare or clean] of the furage [wadding for gun or pistol] and riding forward gripping the horses' bridles in the nearest side and held them still, George Balfour fired likewise, and James Russell got George Fleming's sword and lighted off his horse, and ran to the coach door, and desired the bishop to come forth, Judas. He answered, he never wronged man: James declared before the

Lord that it was no particular interest nor yet for any wrong that he had done to him, but because he had betrayed the church as Judas, and had wrung his hands these 18 or 19 years in the blood of the saints, but especially at Pentland; and Mr Guthrie and Mr Mitchell and James Learmonth; and they were sent by God to execute his vengeance on him this day, and desired him to repent and come forth; and John Balfour on horseback said, Sir, God is our witness that it is not for any wrong thou hast done to me, nor yet for any fear of what thou could do to me, but because thou hast been a murderer of many a poor soul in the kirk of Scotland, and a betrayer of the church, and an open enemy and persecutor of Jesus Christ and his members, whose blood thou hast shed like water on the earth, and therefore thou shalt die! and fired a pistol; and James Russell desired him again to come forth and make him for death, judgment, and eternity; and the bishop said, Save my life, and I will save all yours. James answered, that he knew that it was not in his power either to save or to kill us, for there was no saving of his life, for the blood that he had shed was crying to heaven for vengeance on him, and thrust his shabel at him. John Balfour desired him again to come forth, and he answered, I will come to you, for I know you are a gentleman and will save my life; but I am gone already, and what needs more? And another told him of keeping up of a pardon granted by the king for nine persons at Pentland, and then at the back side of the coach thrust a sword at him, threatening him to go forth; whereupon he went forth, and falling upon his knees, said, For God's sake, save my life; his daughter falling on her knees, begging his life also. But they told him that he should die, and desired him to repent and make for death. Alexander Henderson said, Seeing there has been lives taken for you already, and if ours be taken it shall not be for nought; he rising of his knees went forward, and John Balfour stroke him on the face, and Andrew Henderson stroke him on the hand and cut it, and John Balfour rode him down; whereupon he, lying upon his face as if he had been dead, and James Russell hearing his daughter say to Wallace that there was life in him yet, in the time James was disarming the rest of the bishop's men, went presently to him and cast of his hat, for it would not cut at first, and haked his head in pieces.

Having thus done, his daughter came to him and cursed him, and called him a bloody murderer; and James answered they were not murderers, for they were sent to execute God's vengeance on him; and presently went to the coach, and finding a pair of pistols, took them, and then took out a trunk and brake it up, and finding nothing but women's furniture, and asked what should be done with it; and it was answered, that they would have nothing but papers and arms; and Andrew Henderson lighted, and took a little box and brake it up, and finding some papers, which he took; and opening a cloak-bag they found more papers and a Bible full of porterers [portraits], with a little purse hung in it, a copper dollar, two pistol ball, two turners, two stamps, some coloured thread, and some yellow coloured thing like to pairings of nails, which would not burn, which they took. At this time James Russell was taking the rest of his men's arms, and Wallace, as he would have resisted, came roundly forward, and

72

James Russell smote him on the cheek with his shabel and riped all their pockets, and got some papers and a knife and fork, which he took; and crying to the rest to see that the bishop be dead, William Dalziel lighted, and went and thrust his sword into his belly, and the dirt came out; turning him over, ript his pockets, and found a whinger and knifes conform, with some papers, which he took. James Russell desired his servants to take up their priest now. All this time Andrew Guillan pleaded for his life. John Balfour threatening him to be quiet, he came to Rathillet, who was standing at a distance with his cloak about his mouth all the time on horseback, and desired him to come and cause save his life, who answered, as he meddled not with them nor desired them to take his life, so he durst not plead for him nor forbid them.

Then they all mounted, and going west gathered up some pistols which they had thrown away after fired.

Isabel was the Archbishop's daughter who later married John Cunninghame of the Barns, near Crail.

James Russell accused the Archbishop of having "betrayed the church as Judas, and having wrung his hands these 18 or 19 years in the blood of the saints, but especially at Pentland; and Mr Guthrie and Mr Mitchell and James Learmonth".

In naming PENTLAND Russell was referring to the "Pentland Rising" of 1666 when about 1,000 poorly-armed men from the far south-west marched to Edinburgh to petition the Privy Council. Forced to back away from Edinburgh by the Edinburgh Fencibles, a force of landed vigilantes, they were attacked and defeated at Rullion Green, on the slopes of the Pentlands, by a government force commanded by Tam Dalyell of the Binns. Fifty of the protestors, and they were never a proper threat to the government, were killed and over thirty of the eighty taken prisoner were executed whilst others were banished to Barbados. Covenanters across Scotland believed that the King had recommended leniency but that Archbishop Sharp suppressed the King's letter.

"MR GUTHRIE" was executed soon after the Restoration of King Charles II as a man whose Covenanting past made him a natural enemy of the King.

"MR MITCHELL" was James Mitchell who had made an earlier attempt to assassinate Sharp, in July 1668. Mitchell was caught and imprisoned on the Bass Rock until executed on 18th January 1678. Robert Louis Stevenson's ghost story, "The Tale of Tod Lapraik" (in the novel *Catriona*) is about Covenanting days on the Bass Rock. Russell would have believed that Sharp had hounded Mitchell to his death and had persuaded him to confess to an attempt at murder by promising him his life. There seems to be no doubt that on 11th July 1668 Mitchell waited for Sharp to come to his coach at the head of Blackfriars Wynd, which runs from the High Street to the Cowgate, and when the Archbishop had entered and taken his seat, Mitchell stepped forward and fired a pistol, loaded with three balls, into the coach. Honeyman, Bishop of Orkney, was stepping into the coach when Mitchell fired and he was shot in the wrist whilst the Primate escaped unhurt. Mitchell walked slowly away until he came to Niddry's Wynd when a man tried to stop him but backed off when Mitchell threatened him with his gun. Mitchell continued down the Wynd and into a house in Stevenlaw's Close, today just above Hunter Square at the Tron Kirk, where he changed his clothes and came back out onto the street believing that was the place where he would be least suspected. The Council offered a reward of 5,000 merks but nothing came of that and Mitchell was not captured until early in 1674.

JAMES LEARMONTH was involved in the killing of a soldier, John Hogg, at the Whitekirk conventicle in May 1678 and was executed on 27th September 1678.

THE FOLLOWING IS A LETTER FROM
WILLIAM SHARP, THE ARCHBISHOP'S SON
TO SIR JAMES BAIRD, AT BANFF,
GIVING AN ACCOUNT OF HIS FATHER'S MURDER
FROM ST ANDREWS AND DATED
10TH MAY 1679,
BEFORE HIS FATHER'S FUNERAL
HAD TAKEN PLACE

Honoured Sir,

This horrid and stupendous murther [murder] has so confounded me, that
I am not able to give a suitable return to your excellent and kind letter.
What I have learnt of that execrable deed is, that on Friday the 2nd of this
instant month, my worthy father crossed the water, lay at Kennoway all
night, next morning set out for St Andrews. Being two miles off, 27 of those
villainous regicides had a full view of the coach, and not finding the
opportunity, divided into three parties, which took up the three ways he
could take homewards. Nine of them assaulted the coach within two miles
of this place, by discharging their pistols, and securing his servants. The
coachman drove on for half-a-mile, until one of his horses was wounded in
three places, and the postilion wounded in the hand. Then they fired
several shot at the coach, and commanded my dearest father to come out,
which he said he would. When he had come out, (not being yet wounded)
he said, Gentlemen, I beg my life. No! bloody villain, betrayer of the cause
of Christ, no mercy! Then, said he, I ask none for myself; but have mercy
on my poor child, (his eldest daughter was in the coach with him,) and
holding out his hand to one of them, to get his, that he would spare his
child, he cut him in the wrist. Then falling down upon his knees, and
holding up his hands, he prayed that God would forgive them; and, begging
mercy for his sins from his Saviour, they murdered him, by sixteen great
wounds, in his back, head, and one above his left eye, three in his left hand,
when he was holding them up, with a shot above his right breast, which
was found to be powder. After this damnable deed, they took the papers
out of his pocket, robbed my sister and their servants of all their papers,
gold and money; and one of these hellish rascals cut my sister in the
thumb, when she had him by the bridle, begging her father's life. God of his
infinite mercy support this poor family, under this dreadful and

unsupportable case, and give us to know why God is thus angry with us, and earnestly beg not to consume us in his wrath, but now that his anger may cease, and he may be at peace with us, through the blood of a reconciled Saviour; and also may have pity upon this poor distressed church, and that he may be the Last sacrifice for it, as he is the first protestant martyr bishop in such a way.

Dear Sir, as my worthy father had alway a kindness and particular esteem for your self, son, and family, so I hope you will be friendly to his son, who shall ever continue, worthy sir, your most faithful, &c. &c.

That the murder was not planned and that the murderers rode without an uncoordinated plan is now generally accepted. Certainly there were not twenty-seven men involved and it is very doubtful that the Archbishop prayed as his son believed he did. Also, few historians believe that the Covenanters were interested in stealing "gold and money". That Sharp showed considerable courage whilst being shot at has been generally accepted, but Covenanting writers have liked to believe that when the assassins drew their swords, and Sharp saw cold steel, then his courage failed and "he made hideous schrieichs as ever was heard." A contrast was being drawn here with the exemplary courage shown by the Covenanting martyrs under torture and painful executions. There were reports that the Archbishop's daughter's screams were heard in Magus village.

Whatever individual men and women may have thought of the murder of any man, it is clear that the Covenanters had the support of their communities. They were given shelter and hospitality; no one betrayed them despite the large rewards on offer and the penalties prescribed for helping them. The Fife lairds, farm servants and villagers were as true to the murderers of Sharp as the Highland Jacobites were to Prince Charles Edward Stewart after the battle of Culloden.

ARCHBISHOP JAMES SHARP'S FUNERAL

IN ST ANDREWS ON 17th MAY 1679

FROM THE RUINED CATHEDRAL TO
THE PARISH CHURCH OF THE HOLY TRINITY

The Parish Church of the Holy Trinity, St Andrews, June 2002.

THE FUNERAL of Archbishop James Sharp was not held until Saturday 17th May 1679. He had been murdered on Saturday 3rd May but the preparations for a very grand funeral probably could not have been undertaken more quickly; certainly the Lord Lyon quite surpassed himself. The procession involved, first, sixty black-suited old men, one for each year of Sharp's life, then banners and standards, horses and trumpets. The first dignitaries were magistrates and members of the University of St Andrews who were followed by ministers and doctors, followed by judges and royal officials. Then came the decorated coffin and following it the bishops, nobility and friends and relations. Soldiers lined the route from the ruined Cathedral, where those in the procession gathered and formed ranks, to the door of the Parish Church of the Holy Trinity where the funeral was to take place. Also paraded was the coach in which the Archbishop had been riding when murdered, and on display in that parade of several hundred people was Sharp's blood-stained gown. The government was stating that one man may have died but the King and his Council remained untouched and all-powerful.

The sermon was preached not by the Archbishop of Glasgow, Alexander Burnet, Sharpe's successor at St Andrews who attended the funeral, but by John Paterson, Bishop of Edinburgh. Paterson's sermon was not published and not a page of its contents has survived. The late Archbishop's body may have been buried in the grounds of the cathedral until the grandiose marble monument in Holy Trinity Church was erected when, presumably, the body was placed in the church. The tomb is said to be again empty as in 1725 "certain riotous and disorderlie persons" broke into the church and removed the body.

This Parish Church, or Toun Kirk, has a history that goes back to the twelfth century, but the old church was not consecrated until 1246, by the ever-active Bishop David Bernham. In 1410 land in the centre of the town was given by Sir David Lindsay of the Byres, an ancestor of the Earls of Lindsay, to enable a new church to be built. This was completed in 1412. With the Reformation came John Knox who preached in the Parish Church in June 1559. When Episcopacy came, Archbishop Spottiswoode used Holy Trinity as his "cathedral"; Archbishop Sharp used the church similarly. In 1899 plans were advanced for a restoration of the church and Peter MacGregor Chalmers was given the most important commission of his illustrious career in church work. The church was near enough remade, and re-dedicated in 1909. The great east and west windows, of 1914, have stained glass by Douglas Strachan. In 1926 a chime of fifteen bells was installed in the old tower in memory of Dr Playfair who had been very involved in having the church restored and in having the Playfair Aisle built. It is this church's bell that I listen for as I walk the streets and wynds of St Andrews.

The Sharp monument is very grand; it has to be seen to be appreciated. It may have been made in the Netherlands and is certainly of black and white Greek and Italian marble and shows realistically, in bas-relief, the Archbishop's murder. An arch frames a tomb-chest that sits on three skulls. On the chest Sharp is portrayed praying, with his mitre and pastoral staff put aside. Behind the Archbishop an angel, emerging from a cloud, holds a martyr's golden crown.

The monument was commissioned by his son, Sir William Sharp, and may have been in place as soon as December 1679. It is so high that the roof had to be raised to get it into what was then a communion aisle. Excellent restoration work was done to the monument in the late 1990s. The Latin inscription, in formal capitals, was written by Andrew Bruce, Bishop of Dunkeld. It is a terrible narrative, describing, how he was,

> slaughtered in a terrible manner, having fallen on his knees that he might yet pray for his own people; he was pierced through by very many wounds of pistols, swords and daggers, by nine forsworn parricides excited by fanatical rage in the full sunlight of midday in the vicinity of his own metropolitan city in spite of the tears and protests of his most dear first-born daughter, and of his domestic servants, who had been wounded; on the third day of May, 1679, 61 years of age.

Contemporary engraving of Archbishop James Sharp's murder on Magus Muir
about midday on Saturday 3rd May 1679.

THE ASSASSINS ESCAPING FROM FIFE

AND AT DRUMCLOG AND
THE BATTLE OF BOTHWELL BRIDGE

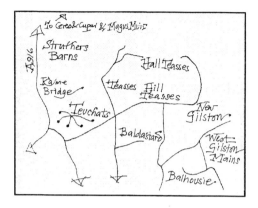

HAVING gathered up some pistols which they had thrown away after firing them, the assassins re-mounted and prepared to leave Magus Muir. As James Russell did so he saw Alexander Leslie of Kennoway approaching, and rode over to ask him to identify himself. He answered that he was one of Archbishop Sharp's servants and, having disarmed him, Russell commanded him to quit his horse and sent him off unharmed on foot. This could have been the servant that Sharp had sent to pay his respects to the Earl of Crawford. The assassins then took up their cloaks which they had thrown off at the east side of Magus, and charging their pistols, discussed where to go. They chose Teuchats, which is about three miles from the scene of the murder, east of today's A916, and in 2002 a bus timetable lists Teuchats Toll as a stopping place. The tenant farmer at Teuchats was James Anderson and his servant, Thomas Cow, seems to have known at least two of the assassins. Tradition has it that the fugitives passed Blackfaulds, near Baldinnie, and skirted the farm of Bruntshiels, and that George Fleming and Andrew and Alexander Henderson washed the blood from their swords at Maul Loch. Teuchats is in an area where many of the farmers were sympathetic to those who had conspired to deal with Carmichael – Baldastard, Hill Teasses and Gilston. We have to remember that this was early afternoon on a sunny day in early May and the assassins must have been very aware of how they must have attracted some attention as they rode around Ceres and Tarvit Hill and that now they were men on the run from a large locally-based army of the King.

As the nine assassins were riding away from Magus Muir they decided that George Balfour should go to Gilston to warn his brothers and Thomas Ness of what had been done, and if they thought it wise they could come to Teuchats to add numbers to see off any soldiers attempting to arrest the murderers. When George Balfour arrived at Teuchats it was to say that his brothers and Ness, astonished to hear of the Archbishop's murder, had refused to join them. The men decided to put up their horses and, placing a man where he could see anyone approaching from any direction, then "went to prayer, first together, then each alone, with great composure of spirit, and enlargement of heart more nor ordinary, blessing the Lord, who had called them out and carried them so courageously through so great a work."

The fugitives ate, fed their horses and looked over the papers they had taken from the Archbishop till about eight o'clock at night when all nine of them rode about half a mile west from Teuchats. There George Fleming, Andrew Henderson and Alexander Henderson parted from the others to go home to Balbuthie and Kilbrackmont. At Devon Common, east of Milldeans and north of today's ruined Bighty, William Danziel broke away to go home to Cadham, probably to go past Ballinkirk and Carriston farms to today's Star village from where he could avoid Markinch by going across the moss to Balfarg near Leslie.

The remaining men turned northwards, perhaps skirting Coaltown of Burnturk, to go down past Priestfield to cross the Eden at Pitlessie bridge. Once over the river they would go past Ramornie and the now-gone Killoch to Edensmuir, that lay to the west of where Ladybank now stands. At Edensmuir it was the turn of Andrew Guillan to leave the others to go home either to Balmerino or somewhere near Falkland.

Edenstown was there when the assassins were making their escape, but Monkston was not built until the old village of Killoch (or Kinloch) was removed early in the nineteenth century. The Kinloch estate of George Balfour lies nearby at Collessie, but to go there would have been too risky even for its reckless owner. The fugitives did not have to skirt Ladybank as that now very sizable village did not exist until the coming of the railway line. The road from Edensmuir to Dunshalt gives open views of the Lomond hills behind Falkland, and the straight road from Dunshalt to Falkland offers other prospects. Within Falkland, the summit of East Lomond can be seen over a variety of roofs.

East Lomond from Falkland, June 2002.

Idealised view of Dura Den, where an extensive collection of fossilised
fish were found in the yellow sandstone. From Swan's engraving of 1890.

Unlike these hurrying fugitives, we can stroll through historic Falkland
or along the burn that runs through Pitlessie to stand by the curving Eden.
Or we can pause near Ladybank to take in a splendid view of the Howe of
Fife; the Lomonds, with historic Falkland at their foot, are further
enhanced by an open panoramic view that allows us to see the villages of
Kingskettle (with the tower of Kettle Church a pleasing landmark),
Kettlebridge (known as Holekettle when the fugitive James Russell lived
there) and Freuchie with another spire rising from the midst of its well-
grouped cottages.

Obviously the movements of the assassins are never going to be
positively known and another version is that they rode three miles to what
became known as the Covenanters' Cave in the sandstone cliff of Dura Den,
near Kemback. Yet another story, seemingly told to the authorities by
William Wallace, one of the Archbishop's two mounted servants, and
Abraham Smith, the Archbishop's coachman, is that Hackston and Balfour
spent the night after the murder at Mortoun, a house which belonged to
Hackston's sister. It was said that whilst the two men were sleeping
Wallace and Smith, and perhaps Alexander Leslie, attempted to break into
Mortoun to take the murderers. It was also said that Smith struggled with
Hackston who broke free and that both men got away. In the house they
found the pistol which had been taken from Wallace and also Hackston's
famous cloak. Nothing was impossible in these violent times and Sharp's

men may have wished to do what they saw as necessary without calling on Carmichael or troopers to go with them to Mortoun and they may have been exceptionally lucky in going to the right house.

The more likely turn of events is that when the remaining four parted from Guillan at Edensmuir they quickly headed west and out of Fife. James Russell's version of the days after the murder has them going towards Bridge of Earn but, thinking that the bridge might be guarded, they did not cross the river but went to a widow's house on the east side of the bridge and stayed there on Sunday, Monday and Tuesday. On Tuesday afternoon they saw a squad of soldiers coming over the bridge from Perth to search the yard. A footman at a nearby house, "being an enemy to the good cause", had seen George Balfour go, with their landlady's brother, to St Johnstone the day before and, spying into who the strangers were, told the soldiers that they were in the house by the waterside. Riding fast away, they turned back to see what the troopers were planning to do before riding to quarters in Abernethy. They did not feel safe there and James Russell and George Balfour rode a mile west to a smiddy to have their horses shod. The smith told them all the latest news, including that Inchdairnie had been killed.

Andrew Aytoun the younger, of Inchdairnie, near Kinglassie, who was about seventeen years of age, was travelling fast on the old road by Leslie to Falkland, or perhaps he was going to Cupar, with his footman and a companion. He knew nothing of the murder of the Archbishop or that the troopers were out looking for the murderers. Catching the flash of steel from fast-riding troopers, he increased his speed and so attracted the attention of the soldiers who followed him, shooting as they closed on the young man. According to Presbyterian historians, the trooper who shot him in the back was named Auchmuty. The wounded man and his companions were taken to Cupar where they were interrogated till Inchdairnie died the following day. His companion, equally innocent, was kept in prison until December 1679. As part of a general round-up of suspects, two men were arrested in Perth on 6th May, one a merchant who had recently arrived in Perth and the other a periwig maker from Strathmiglo; they were not released until 15 July 1679. Others were interrogated but none had anything to do with the murder.

The once very grand Inchdairnie, near Kinglassie, from a drawing of the 1890s. The Aytouns owned the estate from the early sixteenth century.

Amongst those interrogated were James Anderson in Teuchats and his servant Thomas Cow, but that was not until 31st May with the interview taking place in Edinburgh. From the information supplied by Anderson the Privy Council was able to make a list of the nine suspects. In Fife the people of Magus were questioned and they offered confirmation of Anderson's account. After Claverhouse's defeat at Drumclog the murder became less important to the Privy Council and it was not until 20th September that the names of the murderers were issued in a proclamation. Four and a half months had passed since the murder but throughout that time, in London, the King was as concerned with the murder as with the armed rebellion of those who fought at Drumclog and insisted that action should be taken against those who would not acknowledge that the killing of the Archbishop was murder. The aim of this verbal test was to help identify potential murderers amongst the rebels who were taken prisoner.

We cannot know the westerly route taken by the fugitives, although the hill roads to Lindores must have been considered, but perhaps they did not go so far north and preferred to risk passing near Auchtermuchty and Strathmiglo, edging Abernethy and Aberargie as they approached the bridge over the Earn. In the days following the murder the four assassins were constantly moving from house to house: to Dupplin Mill, to the Ochils, and Rathillet to Balvaird and Lindores, staying at the house of Robert Cairns who was not only a friend but free of suspicion. Hackston was, however, "such a terror on the spirits" of the Cairns family that he went back to his own house, where he remained all Sunday before going to a tenant's house where he organised his affairs. Perhaps the fugitive was in Kilmany where today it is difficult to envisage this other than as a place of rural peace.

View from Dysart over the Forth to Inchkeith island and Edinburgh's Arthur's Seat. Photograph 2001.

On Monday Hackston and his man, James Kenneir, rode back to Balvaird where they arrived on Tuesday morning and stayed all day before riding at night to Dupplin Mill before moving on to the "Chingles at Forteviot Church", where he got some rest. He was also at Laurence Duncan's in Aberdalgie Wood. Going to Dupplin Mill on foot to get what news they could, James Russell and George Balfour by chance met Alexander Dunneir who took them to a gentleman's house near Drummond Castle, by Muthill south of Crieff. Once visited by kings and queens, forfeited after the defeat of Charles Edward Stewart and with a murder in the family, today Drummond is visited for its formal garden.

After two or three days the visiting assassins left Drummond to go back to Aberdalgie to keep John Balfour, who seems to have been more relaxed about staying in one place, informed. The others continued to move between various houses and whilst at the Chingles they sent for William Danziel, who had been hiding alone for most of the time in Dysart, in an old house belonging to Mrs Dongel that was some way out of the town. Mrs Dongel and her daughters brought him food during the night. He had spent the first day after the murder in Leslie with James Martin (who had been at a meeting of the conspirators in Leslie on 18th April) and Janet Moses, his wife, but that house had been searched by troopers and soldiers and he was lucky to escape by the back door.

84

Ruined Balvaird Castle, from a drawing of the 1890s, that stands a little
to the east of the road that goes from Gateside to Beinn Inn.

Danziel was able to join the others at the Chingles thanks to Isabel
Alison, of Perth, being willing to travel to Dysart to take him to Perthshire.
This brave woman became a Covenanting martyr, executed on 26th
January 1681 in the Grassmarket, Edinburgh. A follower of Donald Cargill,
during interrogation Alison was asked if she had spoken not only with
Cargill but also with David Hackston, who had been executed on 30th
September 1680. The woman, who knew that she was to be executed,
replied that she did and added, "I bless the Lord that ever I saw him, for I
never saw in him but a godly pious youth." She was also asked about John
Balfour and "the two Hendersons that murdered the Lord St Andrews", to
which she replied, "I never knew any Lord St Andrews. They said Mr
James Sharp, if ye call him so. I never thought it murder; but if God moved
and stirred them to execute his righteous judgment upon him, I have
nothing to say to that."

Gradually the fugitives worked their way west through the Campsies to
Kippen, Fintry and Kilsyth and to Strathaven in Lanarkshire and so to the
momentous events at Drumclog and Bothwell Bridge.

For some five or six days after the murder, George Fleming, son of
George Fleming of Balbuthie, and Andrew and Alexander Henderson, sons
of John Henderson of Kilbrackmont, worked as usual but news reached
them that the soldiers were in the Kilconquhar area tracking them down.
At first they hid locally in caves and, with the soldiers searching
everywhere, they were lucky not to be caught. A popular story is of Andrew
Henderson lying in a little hole and that the troopers and soldiers who
came to the hole close to a farm steading only turned away when their

Kilconquhar Church and loch.

commander shouted to the soldier that was closest to Henderson, "Are you seeking hens?"

When attending a religious meeting at which Cargill preached, Hackston, George Balfour, James Russell, John Balfour, and William Danziel met a James Boog whom they sent to Fife to bring Andrew and Alexander Henderson and George Fleming to Lanarkshire. These three were able to use the experiences of the others to travel via Dupplin Mill and Dunblane to Kilsyth and from there to Arnbuckle and to near Strathaven where they arrived on 3rd June – exactly on time for the events at Drumclog.

The earlier arrivals in Lanarkshire had been involved in national Covenanting affairs that involved extremists: Hackston and John Balfour were in Glasgow to meet Donald Cargill, and William Danziel, James Russell and George Balfour were near Strathaven with a Covenanting force that expected the enemy to attack that night. After a gathering of Covenanters at Rutherglen, when a declaration was nailed to the Mercat Cross, Danziel and James Russell were on sentry duty at Glasgow Bridge to watch the movements of the government forces. Soon the men went to Eaglesham, near Fenwick Moor, and to Newmilns, near Loudon Hill. Reports had indicated that Claverhouse was "rindging all the country" for the Covenanters, and when the encounter with Claverhouse came at Drumclog, a boggy moor near Strathaven, the Covenanters were well prepared. They were commanded by Sir Robert Hamilton and his officers included Robert Fleming, David Hackston and John Balfour.

On that morning, Claverhouse, commanding a regiment of life-guards, advanced from Hamilton up the vale of Avon, bearing with him two

86

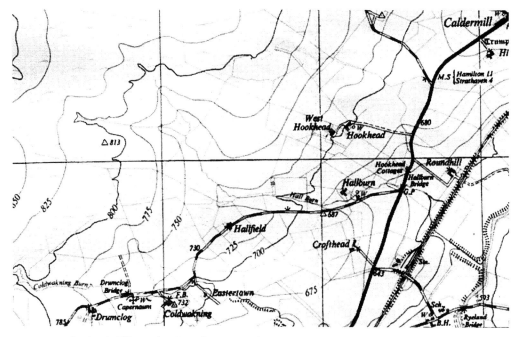

Map showing the hilly terrain at Drumclog, near Strathaven.

field-preachers whom he had seized in the vicinity of the town. He halted at the village of Strathaven, after a ride of seven or eight miles, in order to breakfast. When Claverhouse led his troops against the Covenanters, he did so confidently as the grim Covenanters advanced in good order, singing psalms, but the young commander was unlucky in that a pitchfork badly injured his stallion which bolted, taking Claverhouse with him. Claverhouse described the action in a letter to the Earl of Linlithgow, Commander-in-Chief of King Charles II's forces in Scotland, written in Glasgow on 1st June 1679 immediately after his ignominious retreat from Drumclog, "We keeped our fyre till they were within ten pace of us: they recaived our fire, and advanced to shock; the first they gave us brocht down the Coronet Mr Crafford and Captain Bleith, besides that with a pitchfork they made such an openeing in my rone horse's belly, that his

John Graham of Claverhouse as portrayed in John Howie's *The Scots Worthies*.

Bothwell Bridge from an eighteenth-century engraving.

guts hung out half an elle, and yet he carried me aff an mile; which so discouraged our men, that they sustained not the shock, but fell into disorder."

The Covenanters achieved their famous victory over John Graham of Claverhouse but William Danziel was fatally wounded. He fired twice before "lowping owre the gett among the eneymys" where he received his wound. His horse being "dung back by the strength of the enemy, fell over and dang over James Russell's horse, being upon his right hand, and James presently rose and mounted and pursued, calling to a woman to take up his dear friend William Danziel." When Russell returned from a fast pursuit of the enemy he immediately went looking for his friend and was still with Danziel when he died twenty-four hours later. William Danziel (often known as William Dingwall) was buried on 3rd June 1679 in Strathaven kirkyard where a memorial was erected in 1732 and renewed in 1833. The graveyard is high on a hill overlooking the town.

Following his retreat, and also harassment, at Strathaven, Claverhouse reached Glasgow. In London, where open rebellion may have been welcomed by the King, who remained agitated by Archbishop Sharp's murder, a response was made very quickly. An army was sent under the command of James, Duke of Monmouth, who took command at Bothwell Bridge where the Covenanters were encamped, and much engaged in theological debate, on the south side of the River Clyde, having possession of the bridge. It was at that time a very narrow structure and sloped

88

Bothwell Bridge, from a work by Sir George Reid dated 1886.

steeply up to the centre. The battle took place on Sunday 22nd June, with Claverhouse in command of a troop of cavalry.

A group of 300 men led by James Ure of Shargarton, David Hackston of Rathillet and John Hall of Haughhead defended the bridge as the Royalist army attacked from the north and, despite much bravery, the Covenanters were forced back to the south bank where a bloodbath ensued, although Monmouth stopped the slaughter as quickly as he could. As both man and commander of the Covenanters, Sir Robert Hamilton has been found to be wanting; his uncle Gilbert Burnet saw him as a "crack brained enthusiast, and under the show of hero was an ignominious coward". The Rev. John Blackader, who died on the Bass Rock, wrote of Hamilton at Bothwell Bridge, "I have often heard that the gentleman who did always take the chief command upon himself, to-wit, R. Hamilton, behaved not worthily that day, showing neither courage, conduct nor resolution: but, at best, as a man damned or demented, and also among the foremost that fled." That had to be set against the courage shown repeatedly by Hackston and Balfour of Kinloch.

At Bothwell Bridge the Covenanters lost 400 men and over twelve hundred were taken prisoner and marched to Edinburgh where they endured months of open-air imprisonment. Some died, some escaped, and some were shipped to Barbados as slaves. In *Old Mortality*, Sir Walter Scott used a fictional Grahame who was killed at Drumclog to give dramatic expression to the violent aspect of Claverhouse's character,

. . . even above the din of conflict, exclaiming to his soldiers: "Kill, kill – no quarter – think on Richard Grahame!" The dragoons, many of whom had shared the disgrace of Louden Hill, required no exhortations to vengeance as easy as it was complete. Their swords drank deep of slaughter among the unresisting fugitives. Screams for quarter were only answered by the shouts with which the pursuers accompanied their blows, and the whole field presented one general scene of confused slaughter, flight, and pursuit.

Today's Bothwell bridge is the seventeenth-century bridge widened and improved in 1826 and 1871. It has four spans with ribbed arches; the triangular cutwaters are especially needed here as the Clyde narrows.

Andrew and Alexander Henderson and George Fleming not only survived the skirmish at Drumclog but also the bloodier battle of Bothwell Bridge, escaping to Holland where they remained perhaps till 1688. Following the death of Charles II in 1685, his brother James VII significantly failed to take the Coronation oath to defend the Protestant religion. In May 1685 the Earl of Argyll sailed from Amsterdam to launch an attempt to challenge the new King and it could be that George Fleming and John Balfour both fought for him. Like his father, Argyll, who was beheaded, died with great courage, and so did many of his supporters who suffered much in prison, but it seems that George Fleming lived to become a respected elder of the kirk. In some ways his father suffered greater penalties than he did, as did John Henderson, father of Andrew and Alexander, who was imprisoned, heavily fined and had soldiers quartered on him. George Fleming, senior, suffered similarly and the parish of Kilconquhar paid £8,500 for its support for the Covenanting cause.

James Russell of Kettle, although less renowned than Hackston and Balfour, was a complex fanatic. His account of the murder and of the escaping murderers is wordy and lacks the drama of John Knox's account of the murder of Cardinal Beaton, but he seems to have written truthfully and with less intent to falsify the evidence than his contemporary Episcopalians and later historians from both sides of what was to the Covenanters a civil war. We have glimpsed Russell beside Danziel at Drumclog and he survived Bothwell Bridge to escape to Holland but, astonishingly, within a few months he was back in Scotland and in 1681 pinned on the door of Kettle Parish Church a vituperative protest which was also printed as folio sheets. He was to be described by his fellow members of the suffering Remnant as "a man of a hot and fiery spirit" who bred confusion in the assembly through his strict questioning of matters relating to any base compliance with law that Russell held in abomination. At another meeting Russell gave a paper "replete with bitterness, untenderness and reflections" and followed this statement with another publication. Generally Russell quarreled with his fellow members of the Remnant, including James Renwick, and retreated to Groningen where he kept up the schism. Soon this fanatical man of Kettle disappears from our view, having left Groningen, and how or where he died is unknown.

Detail, much reduced, from Sir David Wilkie's "Pitlessie Fair", 1804.

Unlike the young David Hackston in Rathillet, I cannot see James Russell getting dressed in his finest Sunday best to walk from Kettlebridge to Pitlessie to join in the high-jinks of the fair which David Wilkie, from near by Kirkton of Cults, fixed in colourful pigments.

At Bothwell Bridge, as at Drumclog, John Balfour showed again that he was a natural fighter, being one of the last to leave the scene of the battle. After his heroic minutes at Bothwell a wounded Balfour disappears into the shadows of legend as a crazed figure on wild moors and soaring rock faces; almost a King Lear of the Fife lairds. Sir Walter Scott invented a history for Balfour in *Old Mortality* where he appears under the name of Burley,

> Burley, only altered from what he had been formerly by the addition
> of a grisly beard, stood in the midst of the cave with his clasped
> Bible in one hand and his drawn sword in the other. His figure,
> dimly ruddied in the red light of the red charcoal, seems that of a
> fiend in the lurid atmosphere of Pandemonium.

That is pure fiction, but there have been many other writers who have confidently given details of what Balfour did after Bothwell Bridge. To take some examples: it could be that after the Battle of Bothwell Bridge the real-life Balfour did hide amongst his Covenanting brethren before escaping to Holland; it could be that he joined the service of the Prince of Orange who became King of England, Scotland and Ireland; it could be that, with George Fleming, he did fight with Argyll against the army of James VII. It could also be that, true fanatic, he decided to return to Scotland to continue the fight against those he regarded as persecuting "the Lord's cause and the people of Scotland", and died at sea before the ship he sailed on reached port. Or, it could be that he did go back to Collessie and hid in a cottage deep in the hills. Balfour may have been glimpsed peering out from his new home, cave or cottage, with his broad bearded face dramatised by staring eyes that indicated the madness brought on him by memories of a blood-stained Magus Muir or the wild charges of Drumclog and Bothwell. If he was recognized, not one parishioner informed on him despite the 10,000 merks on his head, as also on that of his brother-in-law, David Hackston. I would suggest that it is more likely from what we know of him that Balfour did not suffer from a sense of guilt or a Learian madness but remained an uncomplicated fighting man. I cannot see him as a Norman Leslie who was haunted by memories of the murder of Cardinal Beaton.

Having fought and led his troop of horse with great courage at Bothwell Bridge, David Hackston escaped into hiding and joined the persuasive Richard Cameron, once of Falkland and a youthful attender at conventicles in the Lomond Hills. None of the Covenanters surpassed Cameron in extremism. With his small band of religious fanatics, who were excluded by their more moderate brethren, he took to the hills with a price on his head. Again there was no betrayal. On 22nd June 1680 Cameron and twenty followers rode through the village of Sanquhar, "with drawn swords and pistols in their hands" to make a Declaration that rejected Charles II as a king who had been "tyrannising on the throne of Britain". That wild and idealistic declaration of open war stirred the blood of generations of so-called hard-headed Lowland Scots.

Cameron House, at the south-west corner of The Cross, Falkland, which is said to be the birthplace of Richard Cameron, who was a schoolmaster in Falkland and, before leaving to be a radical Covenanter, precenter in the Kirk, then Episcopal.
At one time the Hackstons of Rathillet had a house in Falkland, once the precincts of the Court. As Æ. J. G. Mackay suggested, "just as cathedral towns have produced the most vehement Dissenters, so the most determined anti-Royalists were bred in the vicinity of the palace."
Photograph June 2002.

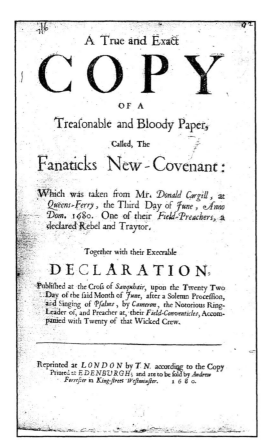

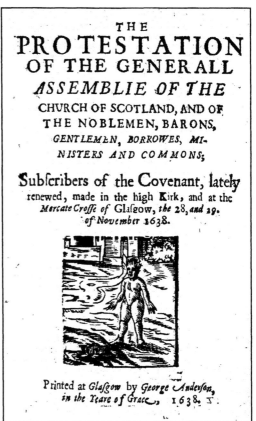

Title-pages of: a reprint of the *Fanaticks New-Covenant* and the Sanquhair Declaration of 1680; and of the earlier "Protestation" against Charles I's religious policies issued by the Covenanters' General Assembly in November 1638.

Hackston may have been one of these wild horsemen who rode between the low thatched cottages of Sanquhar and we know for certain that on 22nd July 1680 he was taken prisoner at a battle fought at Airds Moss, near Muirkirk in Ayrshire. It was about four o'clock when a body of troops led by Sir Andrew Bruce of Earlshall near Leuchars, ("The Bloody Bruce", the "Fife Persecutor") closed in on a gathering of Cameronians. Facing 120 government dragoons, Cameron prayed, in effect, for a good death but Hackston may have been less fatalistic. A contemporary writer counted sixty-three Cameronians; twenty-three horse and forty foot. Cameron attempted to lead his men onto high ground but they soon turned to face the enemy with eight horse on the right, fifteen on the left, with the foot, who were poorly armed, in the middle. Both bodies advanced and a strong party of Bruce's horse came hard at the Cameronians; their horse fired, killing and wounding several Cameronians, both horse and foot, who then advanced to the enemy's "very faces", with Hackston in the front. Seeing the horse behind him breaking, he rode in amongst Bruce's troops and out again without being wounded. He fought on, back and forwards, but ended stuck in a bog, where he was attacked by a man he recognized, David

Earlshall from a drawing of the 1840s by R. W. Billings.

Ramsay, and there both men, now on foot, fought with small swords, without either being able to strike a wounding blow. Soon Hackston was struck down by three mounted dragoons who came behind him and he fell under three severe wounds to the head. Ramsay saved Hackston's life by taking him, bleeding badly, prisoner.

Cameron had been killed and his head and hands were cut off and taken to Edinburgh where they were displayed on Edinburgh's Netherbow Port. As was said at the time. "there's the head and hands that lived praying and preaching, and died praying and fighting".

David Hackston, with the other prisoners, was taken to Douglas where a woman, Janet Cleland, brought a surgeon to tend to his wounds but, fearing retribution, he only staunched the blood. On the next day, in Lanark, he was questioned by General Tam Dalyell of the Binns and Lord Ross, but refused to cooperate. General Dalyell threatened to "roast him alive" but relented and had him tied up and thrown into the tolbooth. Hackston was then taken to Edinburgh and up the High Street to Parliament Close, mounted bareback on a horse, facing backwards, with Cameron's head carried before him on a halberd. The other three prisoners were denied even the status of facing a horse's tail and were "laid on a goad [bar] of iron".

The wounded Hackston was brought immediately before the Council, and again on the 26th June, and before the Judiciary on the 27th when he "declined the King's authority". Clearly an exceptionally brave man amongst many brave Covenanting martyrs, Hackston refused to recognise the authority of the court that tried him and never wavered in his beliefs. He was brought to trial on the 29th July 1680, and again on Friday 30th

94

when, seated, he received his sentence. On being asked if he had more to say, he stated that they were all murderers and that "oppression, perjury, and bloodshed were to be found in their skirts." He was then carried from the bar and drawn backwards on a hurdle to the place of execution at the Cross of Edinburgh. As sentenced by the court, he was allowed to pray but not to speak to the people. On the scaffold his right hand was cut off and, as specifically sentenced, after a long pause, his left was also cut off; all of which he suffered with "great firmness and constancy". Then, to quote a Presbyterian historian who did not write for the squeamish,

> Hackston was drawn up to the top of the gallows with a pulley, and suffered to fall down a considerable way upon the lower scaffold, three time with his whole weight, and then fixed at the top of the gallows. Then the executioner, with a large knife, cut open his breast and pulled out his heart, before he was dead, for it moved when it fell on the scaffold. He then stuck his knife in it and showed it on all sides to the people, crying, "Here is the heart of a traitor". At that he threw it into a fire prepared for that purpose; and having quartered his body, his head was fixed on the Nether Bow, one of his quarters with his hands, at St Andrews, another at Glasgow, a third at Leith, and the fourth at Burntisland.

Later Hackston's hand was taken from St Andrews to Cupar to be displayed there.

Headstone in Cupar Kirkyard. Photograph April 2002.

Following Cameron's death, Donald Cargill, another leader of the strict Covenanters, continued the struggle against the laws of King Charles II. Having excommunicated the King and his brother James, Cargill was taken prisoner at Covington Mill, Lanarkshire, on 12th July 1681 and executed in Edinburgh on 27th July. Andrew Pitulloch and Lawrence Hay were two of his three followers who were executed on 13th July for "denying lawful authority, calling the king a tyrant, and thinking it lawful to kill him." Tradition has it that Lawrence Hay was a weaver from Kilconquhar and Andrew Pitulloch a farmworker from Largo. Their heads were sent to Cupar to be displayed with Hackston's hand. So it is that in Cupar kirkyard a headstone carries two heads, an open right hand and their names as well as that of David Hackston,

> Here lies Interred the Heads of LAURCe HAY
> and ANDREW PITULLOCH who
> suffered martyrdom at EDINr July 13 1681
> for adhering to the word of God, & Scotlands
> covenanted work of Reformation, and also
> one of the Hands of DAVID HACKSTON
> of Rathillet who was most cruelly murdered
> at EDINr July 30th 1680
> for the same cause

On the reverse is inscribed,

Headstone in Cupar Kirkyard commemorating Hay, Pitulloch and Hackston.
Photograph April 2002.

1680

Our persecutors fill'd with rage
their brutish fury to aswage
took heads & hands of martyrs off
That they might be the peoples scoff,
They Hackstons body cutt asunder
And set it up a worlds wonder
In several places to proclaim
these monsters gloryd in their shame.
            Re Erected   July 13 1792.

David Hackston died as a rebel who fought at Drumclog, Bothwell Bridge and Airds Moss as much as for being involved in Archbishop Sharp's murder and, of the nine men who were on Magus Muir, only Andrew Guillan was executed for that murder, and he had wished the Archbishop to be spared. Guillan was very unlucky to be arrested.

Soon after the murder, he thought it best to leave Fife and some four years later he was working in Cockpen, a few miles south-east of Edinburgh, where he refused to attend the parish church and, on being questioned by the Episcopalian minister, refused to recognise his authority. In the village he refused to drink the King's health and was taken first to Dalkeith prison and then to Edinburgh where he was put in the "iron house", a room on the second floor of the Tolbooth, and chained to a bar. There may have been a suspicion that he was involved in the Archbishop's murder as, when questioning Guillan, the advocate mentioned the terrible murder and said how evil it was for the Archbishop to have been murdered while on his knees praying. The righteous Guillan, remembering how Sharp screamed but did not pray, protested, "he would not pray one word for all that could be said to him." This clearly repudiates what is stated on the Sharp monument in Holy Trinity Church and in the Criminal Letters that were raised by Sir George Mackenzie of Rosehaugh in April 1683,

> and his Grace having opened the door, and come forth, and fallen down on his knees, begging mercy, or time to recommend his soul to God, and to pray for his murderers, so cruel and inhumane were they, that without pitying his gray hairs, or the shrieks of his weeping daughter, or respecting his character or office, most cruelly and furiously gave him many bloody and mortal wounds in his head and other places, and left him dead and murdered on the place; and then went into the west, and rose in rebellion at Bothwell Bridge, under the command of the said Robert Hamilton. And when, by the diligence of his majesty's forces, they could no longer stay in the nation, they fled to the United Provinces of Holland . . . .

Guillan was charged with the murder and at his trial on 18th July 1683 was found guilty and sentenced to be taken to the Cross of Edinburgh on Friday 20th July. Before being hanged, both his hands were cut off at the foot of the gallows. His head was taken to Cupar for public display and his body to Magus Muir where it was hung in chains. Some of his friends seem to have been brave enough to take Guillan's body down as the records of the Council 27th May 1684 have a sentence that involved banishment for a crime related to the body.

Guillan's grave was marked at Claremont Farm, near the site of the murder, by a headstone which informed, "The Grave Ston of Andreu Gullin who Suffred at the Gallowlee of Edinburgh July 1683 & afterwards was hung upon a pol in Magus Muir and lyeth hiar."

There is a certain aptness in that Claremont was once the estate of George Martine (1635-1712), Archbishop Sharp's secretary and companion, who wrote an early book on the Archbishopric of St Andrews entitled *Reliquiæ Divi Andræ*. A lawyer and commissary clerk of St Andrews, he lived in South Court, South Street, St Andrews, and his coat of arms is on the wall above the entrance to this interesting court.

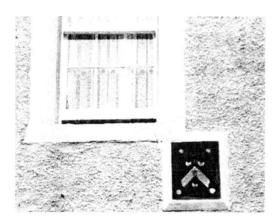

George Martine's coat of arms.

Although Guillan's stone is the only one erected near Magus Muir for a man who witnessed the killing, there is a monument to five other Covenanters who died as a result of the murder. The five Covenanters hanged at Magus Muir were probably nowhere near that spot when the Archbishop was murdered but examples had to be made. These Fife men were amongst the prisoners taken after the defeat of the Covenanting force at Bothwell Bridge. On 26 July King Charles ordered nine of the recently arrested rebels who were thought to have been associated with the murderers to be executed and hanged in chains at the site of Sharp's murder.

The five men who were hanged had refused to swear to be of good behaviour and were brought to trial. They refused even to admit that the killing of the Archbishop was murder and the court found them guilty of murder "after the fact". They were brought to Magus Muir in chains which were still on them when they were hanged. The date was 25th November 1679 and, as the inscription on the stone informs, "Here lies Thos Brown, James Wood, Andrew Sword, John Weddell & John Clyde who suffered martyrdom on Magus Muir for their adherence to the Word of God and Scotland's Covenanted Work of Reformation".

Covenanters' Memorial at Magus Muir. Photograph April 2002.

The words on the other face of the stone are,

> Cause we at Bothwel did appear
> Perjurious Oths refus'd to swear
> Cause we Christ's Cause would not condemn
> We were sentenc'd to Death by Men
> Who Rag'd againsy us in such fury
> Our dead bodies they did not bury;
> But upon Poles did hing us high
> Triumph's of Babel's Victory.
> Our Lives we fear'd not to the Death.
> But consatant prov'd to the last breath.
> Renewed 1872

The road at Magus Muir where the Archbishop was murdered no longer exists. The site of the murder is now within a wood and the memorial erected to mark it is reached by a well-made path. Within a few yards of this memorial is another marking the graves of the five Covenanters who were brought to Magus Muir to be hanged and to "expiate and appease the Archbishop's ghost". Today at the site of Magus Muir the path forms a circular route to and from the monuments. Going by the right-hand section of the path allows Archbishop Sharp's memorial to be approached first. The left-hand path goes through the wood and round to a stone wall edging a cultivated field. The crops vary but Covenanting historians have liked to describe the place on the moor where the five men were hanged as having become a bountiful cornfield. There is a gate in the wall to allow access to the short path to the burial place of the hanged Covenanters. The headstone is surrounded by a 2-foot high stone wall

Monument to mark the place where Archbishop Sharp was murdered.
Photograph April 2002.

topped by iron railings that show only a little rusting. The memorial stone
stands in the centre of this area. The narrow path continues, allowing the
poem on the back of the stone to be read.

Back in the wood, the main path continues round a few yards to the
site of Archbishop Sharp's murder, marked by a memorial which
provides an ideological contrast to the nearby graves of the Covenanters.
The rugged stones of this pyramid must rise to 12 feet and each face is
8 feet in width. The light-coloured slab bearing the inscription contrasts
with the heavy and vigorously cut old reddish-brown stones into which it is
set. The relief lettering on the inscription panel has been damaged and
some of this look like vandalism, especially the letters that form the
Archbishop's name. The formal inscription is in Latin, which has been
translated as: "Near this place James Sharp Archbishop of St Andrews was
murdered by savage enemies in the presence and despite the prayers of his
daughter A.D. 1679".

This was an exposed and treeless moor when the murder took place.
Today, when out of the wood and by the graves in the field, the B939 to
Pitscottie and Cupar can be seen beyond the long slope of the field and
parts of Strathkinness village are visible on the slopes of its small hill.
Looking straight over the gravestone, and across the fields of varied greens,
a large farm, sheltered by a scattering of trees, seems isolated within these
expansive acres. With typical Anglicising perversity, the modern Ordnance
Survey map gives one farm as Upper Magus and another as Nether

Magask. The paths have been recently re-made and cleared of enclosing trees and shrubs, but this can be a lonely walk through an enclosing wood and I would recommend that two or more is good company here.

When Sir Walter Scott took a coach journey past Magus Muir he scared his fellow passengers by retailing the story of the murder. Later a young Robert Louis Stevenson became excited by tales of Magus Muir and when, as a boy, he rode over the Muir with his father he was tense with excitement as the place was approached. As an adult, the story of the murder haunted Stevenson's imagination and the dominant image that he saw was of David Hackston sitting very still as a spectator of murder. He wrote, "the figure that always fixed my attention was that of Hackston of Rathillet sitting in the saddle with his cloak about his mouth. . . . It is an old temptation with me to pluck away that cloak and to see the face; to open that bosom and read the heart."

When Stevenson saw Magus Muir he may have been on his way to Anstruther where his father built a new harbour, and I like to think that father and son went eastwards along the coast past Crail to Fife Ness. And there they would see the old "natural" harbour at the very edge of Fife where once a Frenchwoman, Mary of Guise, came ashore to be married by David Beaton to James V, King of Scots. She became Regent of Scotland and also the great-great grandmother of Charles II, King of Scots, who could not understand that his Scottish subjects were of a nation where speaking one's mind and refusing to act against one's conscience were inbred and treasured values. We may term such values Calvinistic, but they are what motivated Robert Burns, who sang in his great cantata, "Love and Liberty",

> *Liberty's* a glorious feast!
> Courts for cowards were erected
> Churches built to please the priest.

Old "natural" harbour at Fife Ness, April 2002.

Bibliography

ANONYMOUS *A Cloud of Witnesses,* first edition 1714, edition of 1871 edited by John Thomson.

BLACKADER, JOHN *Memoirs,* edited by Andrew Crichton, 1823.

BOWER, WALTER *Scotichronicon,* in Latin and English, vol 8, books 15 and 16, edited by D. E. R. Watt, 1987.

BUCKROYD, JULIA *The Life of James Sharp Archbishop of St Andrews 1618-1679. A Political Biography,* 1987.

BURLEIGH, J. H. S. *A Church History of Scotland,* 1960.

CALDERWOOD, DAVID *The History of the Kirk of Scotland,* edited by Thomas Thomson, 8 vols, 1842-49.

CAMPBELL, THORBJÖRN *Standing Witnesses. A guide to the Scottish Covenanters and their Memorials with a Historical Introduction,* 1996.

CANT, RONALD G. *The Parish Church of The Holy Trinity, St Andrews,* 1992.

CUNNINGHAM, ANDREW S. *Kennoway and the Fringes of Markinch,* 1906.

GEDDIE, JOHN *The Fringes of Fife,* 1894, new edition [1927].

GIFFORD, JOHN *The Buildings of Scotland: Fife,* 1988, reprinted with corrections, 1992 and reprinted 2000.

GLEN, DUNCAN *Splendid Lanarkshire,* 1997.

——*Illustrious Fife,* 1998.

HOWIE, JOHN *The Scots Worthies,* revised by W. H. Carslaw, [1871].

KIRKTON, JAMES *The True and Secret history of the Church of Scotland from the Restoration to the Year 1678. To which is added an account of the Murder of Archbishop Sharp by James Russell, an actor therein,* edited from the MSS by Charles Kirkpatrick Sharpe, Edinburgh, 1817. There is an edition edited by R. Stewart, 1992, but I have not seen it.

KNOX *John Knox's History of the Reformation in Scotland,* edited by William Croft Dickson, vol 1, 1949.

LAMONT, JOHN *Diary, 1649-1671,* edited by G. R. Kinloch, 1830.

LEIGHTON, JOHN M. *History of the County of Fife,* 1840. With Swan's engravings.

LINDSAY *The Works of Sir David Lindsay of the Mount 1490-1555,* edited by Douglas Hamer, 4 vols, 1931-36.

LINDSAY OF PITSCOTTIE *The Historie and Chronicles of Scotland,* edited by Aeneas J. G. MacKay, 3 vols, 1899-1911.

LYNCH, MICHAEL *Scotland: A New History,* revised paperback edition 1992.

MACKAY, Æ. J. G. *A History of Fife and Kinross,* 1896.

MACKIE, J. D. *A History of Scotland,* 1964, revised and edited by Bruce Lenman and Geoffrey Parker, 1978, latest reprint 1991.

MILLAR, A.H. *Fife, Pictorial and Historical,* 2 vols, Cupar, 1895.

PATERSON, RAYMOND CAMPBELL *A Land Afflicted. Scotland and the Covenating Wars 1638-1690,* 1998.

PRIDE, GLEN L. *The Kingdom of Fife: An Illustrated Architectural Guide,* 1990.

SANDERSON, MARGARET H. B. *Cardinal of Scotland: David Beaton c.1494-1546,* 1986.

SHARP "Excerpts from the Household Book of My Lord Archbishop of St Andrews from 1663 to 1666 written by George Martine of Claremont", *Miscellany of the Maitland Club,* vol 2, 1840.

SIBBALD, SIR ROBERT *The History Ancient & Modern of Fife & Kinross,* new edition, 1803.

The Statistical Account of Scotland, 1791-1799, reprint of Fife parishes, 1978.

WILKIE, JAMES *Bygone Fife: From Culross to St Andrews,* 1931.

WILKIE, JAMES *Bygone Fife: North of the Lomonds,* 1938.

WODROW, ROBERT *The History of the Sufferings of the Church of Scotland from the Restoration to the Revolution,* edited by Robert Burns, 4 vols, 1828-30.

WOOD, REV. WALTER *The East Neuk of Fife,* second edition, 1887.

WYNTOUN *The Original Chronicle of Andrew of Wyntoun,* edited by F. J. Amours, 1903-14.

Index